American Architecture

American Architecture

AN ILLUSTRATED HISTORY

ROBIN LANGLEY SOMMER WITH PHOTOGRAPHS BY BALTHAZAR KORAB

CRESCENT BOOKS
NEW YORK • AVENEL

Page 1: *A late nineteenth-century house in the fashionable Queen Anne style.*

Page 2: *Frank Lloyd Wright's residential masterpiece Fallingwater (1937), Bear Run, Pennsylvania.*

Right: *The historic Wainwright Building (1891) by Louis Sullivan in St. Louis, Missouri.*

This 1996 edition published by Crescent Books, distributed by Random House Value Publishing, Inc. 40 Engelhard Avenue, Avenel, New Jersey 07001

Random House
New York • Toronto • London • Sydney • Auckland

Produced by Saraband Inc, PO Box 0032, Rowayton, CT 06853-0032
PF CS
Copyright © 1996 Saraband Inc.

Design © Ziga Design
All photographs © Balthazar Korab, unless indicated otherwise in the illustration credits at the end of this book.

A CIP catalog record for this book is available from the Library of Congress

ISBN 0-517-16020-X
DS
10 9 8 7 6 5 4 3 2 1

Printed in China

FOR KEITH, MARC, NICK, AND ANNIE

CONTENTS

INTRODUCTION

Right: *Plains Indian tipis used by nomadic hunting tribes were made of painted hide stretched over a portable wooden framework.*

Below: *Anasazi ruins at Mesa Verde, Colo., built between AD 700 and 1000.*

The long, multifaceted, and dynamic history of the United States is embodied in its architecture, from the woodland shelters and earth-walled pueblos of America's first people to the suburban complexes and skyscrapers of the present day. Perhaps nowhere else have such disparate geographic and cultural forces come into play to form the manmade landscape of a nation.

A complete history of American architecture would fill a bookcase, but one may form a strong impression of this fascinating subject from this pictorial survey through the sensitive photographs of Balthazar Korab, whose experience as an architect is reflected in his pictures. The reader may also discover how much he or she already knows from long familiarity with American neighborhoods, public buildings, houses of worship, and monuments. We are a mobile and adaptive people who have transplanted and modified many styles to suit changing needs, construction materials, and financial factors over time. Ethnic and geographic origins play an important part in recognizing and responding to such distinctive styles as the French Colonial, Gothic Revival, Neoclassic, and regional vernacular. Unlike other art forms, which may appear to be the province of an expert elite, architecture is available to everyone. In essence, it is human shelter.

The dwellings constructed for thousands of years by the Native American peoples evolved from climatic conditions, lifestyles, and available materials. They were of two basic types: wood-frame and earth-wall construction. Wood-frame shelters of the rounded type, like the familiar tipi of the Plains Indians, were readily portable, designed to meet the

needs of nomadic hunters. More elaborate, rectangular wood-frame houses were built by agricultural people like the Iroquois, who lived in permanent or semipermanent communities. Where wood was scarcer, as in the arid West, earth-wall construction evolved, ranging from the simple rounded dugout or hogan to the multilevel, flat-roofed pueblos built high above surrounding farmlands in the shelter of cliff walls. Gathering tribes, like those of California and the inhospitable plateau region, built shelters of reeds (wickiups) and other natural materials that were easily replaceable as the tribe moved on.

Variations on the rounded wood-frame shelter included the wigwam, covered with slabs of bark or mats, and the thatch-covered dwellings of the Wichita. Rectangular wooden dwellings with gabled roofs (plankhouses) were and are built by Northwestern peoples and ornamented with totemic symbols.

In the subtropical Southeast, the Seminole chickee, with its open sides and thatched roof, provided both venti-

Top: Native American women construct a framework for the mat-covered shelter called the wickiup.

Above: The multilevel flat-roofed complex of Taos Pueblo, constructed of adobe on a timber frame.

Left: Ladders provide access to the various levels of Pueblo dwellings.

7

Above: *A typical Midwestern log house built by settler Johannes Eby in 1857 according to Germanic customs of construction. Michigan's Monroe County Historical Society has preserved this example at the county fairgrounds.*

lation and shelter from heavy rainfall and the sun's heat. Sometimes it was raised above the ground on stilts to guard against marauding animals and poisonous insects.

Some features of the indigenous shelters were adopted by European colonists, beginning with the first permanent settlements in the early seventeenth century. More commonly, the Europeans imported stylistic elements from their homelands and adapted them to local conditions as they could. Settlers in the coastal communities had access to a greater variety of building materials and

embellishments, as bulky materials could be transported by water. Others were restricted to simpler folk-style houses until the advent of the railroads in the nineteenth century.

The heavily forested Eastern half of the country was settled primarily by French and English colonists who were familiar with wooden building in the post-and-girt style—frameworks of hewn timber covered by thinner strips of wood. In New England, houses of this kind were usually several rooms deep and several stories high, with a central chimney. Due to the severity of regional winters, they often had connected barns and outbuildings. The more temperate climate of the Tidewater South produced a simpler type of frame folk house, often only one room deep, with the chimney at the gable end. Perhaps the most familiar form of frontier folk house is the log cabin, or Midland style, derived from the log houses built by settlers from central and northern Europe.

As settlement extended farther west, where wood was scarcer, settlers drew upon the native vernaculars to construct the sod houses of the Great Plains and

Right: *An idealized picture of nineteenth-century frontier life. The shed-roofed porch raised on supports shows the influence of French settlers in the vast Illinois Country and Louisiana Territory.*

Left: The U.S. Capitol Building in Washington, D.C. was begun in 1793 to the designs of amateur architect William Thornton, who had won the competition for the design in a field of seventeen entrants. When he proved unqualified to construct the building, French architect Stephen Hallet, the runner-up, was employed. Hallet was only the second of half a dozen major architects involved in the building's construction, reconstruction (after the War of 1812), renovation, and expansion over a 200-year period.

Overleaf: New York City's World Trade Center (1973), twin towers designed by Minoru Yamasaki in association with Emery Roth and Sons. The Brooklyn Bridge is in the foreground.

the flat-roofed adobe houses of the Hispanic Southwest. Where stone was plentiful, it served as a rugged and enduring building material, or provided foundations for houses of wood-frame construction.

The dwellings of Native Americans and frontier settlers alike were constructed according to knowledge and techniques passed down through the generations and modified with the advent of newly adopted technologies or the migration to new environments. These dwellings were conceived and built by their users. In the original thirteen colonies, America made its first contribution to art history in architecture, in the conventional sense of employing specialized, professionally trained designers to create plans and supervise their execution. The classically based Georgian style imported from England predominated.

Thomas Jefferson's later designs for Monticello (begun 1769) and for the University of Virginia (1825) modified the plain Palladian style of early plantation houses along Roman lines. The new Classic Revival style was widely employed for both public and residential buildings from the Revolutionary War well into the 1800s. It comprised both the post-Colonial Federal style, based on Roman prototypes, and the Greek Revival style, based on Greek principles. The Gothic Revival style was also widely accepted by the early 1800s.

The engineering revolution ushered in by industrialization brought another important development in the second half of the nineteenth century: a much simpler and more functional architecture based on iron (later, steel) frameworks. Strong, but light, metal framing made possible the extended use of glass, and

standardization of structural elements increased the speed and economy of construction. These innovations would culminate in a new aesthetic for public buildings during the 1900s. Chicago architect Louis Sullivan became a pioneer of modern architecture with such designs as the Carson, Pirie & Scott Department Store (1904), in which the steel frame itself became a part of the design.

Sullivan's concern with organic form was shared by his disciple, Frank Lloyd Wright, who became perhaps the single most influential force on twentieth-century design. It is a curious fact that both men were products of the romantic Victorian age, with its wide variety of styles, from Italianate and Octagon to the indigenous Stick, Shingle, and Romanesque Revival. Even as Classicism and the various revivals, from Chateauesque to Beaux Arts Eclectic, were having their day (1880s–1940s), Wright and his mentor were breaking new ground. Wright's seventy-year career, which ended only with his death in 1959,

saw concentration on clean, sharply accented lines, flowing interior spaces, and total integration of building and site.

European architects like Walter Gropius, founder of the German Bauhaus movement, shared Wright's belief that a building's form should follow its function, but they brought a different interpretation when they emigrated to the United States with the advent of Nazism. Both Gropius and his Bauhaus associate Mies van der Rohe were dedicated to the concept of pure form and line that came to be known as the International Style. New York City's Seagram's Building (1956) is a well-known example, with its bronze and glass façade raised on piers in an open space—a symbol of modern technology and commercial wealth. In recent years, contemporary architects have challenged what some see as the impersonality of the International Style in many innovative ways. Their contributions are rising alongside those of their predecessors to enrich the complex manmade landscape of the United States and add a new chapter to its exciting architectural history.

Left: Detail of the World Trade Center towers at ground level.

Below: S.R. Crown Hall (1956) is part of the unified group of buildings designed by Mies van der Rohe over a twenty-year period for Chicago's Illinois Institute of Technology (originally the Armour Institute).

THE COLONIAL STYLES

Colonial architecture in North America evolved from European styles of the late Middle Ages and the early Renaissance, modified to meet the needs of the first settlers, most of whom came to the Eastern Seaboard.

The Spanish Colonial style dominated in the Southwest and Florida, where St. Augustine, founded in 1565, is the nation's oldest city. Spanish colonists used the adobe construction techniques that had originally come to Spain from North Africa to build primarily single-story dwellings with asymmetrical façades and tiled roofs, usually enclosing a patio or courtyard. Thick masonry walls of adobe brick or rubble stone, customarily covered with stucco, under a low-pitched roof or a flat roof with parapet, are typical of this style. In the Southwest, Native American pueblo construction techniques were freely adapted by the colonists to the similar Spanish style. Churches and public buildings were constructed in the same materials on a more massive scale, with arches, colonnades, and ornamentation that reflect the Moorish influence on Old Spain.

After the founding of Jamestown, Virginia, in 1607, the English formed the largest group of colonists. They settled the coastal plain extending from what is now Maine to the southern part of present-day Georgia. During the 1600s, postmedieval influences dominated their architecture, characterized by steeply pitched roofs, gables, second-floor overhangs (jetties), large stacked chimneys, and small casement windows, often diamond-paned. The ecclesiastical influence on the Gothic-style architecture is apparent in the pointed arches over doors and windows and in interior vaulting. These features would later inspire the Gothic Revival style and influence the indigenous Stick style as well as the Queen Anne, Richardsonian Romanesque, and Tudor.

The second-floor overhang common during this period added structural stability to timber framing, and windows had small panes because glass—where it was available—was only a recent innovation in the early seventeenth century. Medieval "wind-holes," from which we derive the word window, were simply openings to provide air and emit smoke from interior fires. When ventilation was not required, these openings were covered with skins, fabric, or solid wooden sashes or shutters. Light was admitted by covering the window frame with translucent oiled cloth or paper instead of solid shutters.

Such windows were common in early Colonial America, but as glazing techniques improved in Europe and were imported to the colonies, window sashes

Below: The Spanish Colonial style combined European masonry building techniques with the indigenous adobe construction of the Southwestern pueblo peoples. The Mission Church of San Francisco de Asis in Rancho de Taos, N.M., exemplifies this blend.

were glazed with many small panes of glass, square or diamond-shaped, held in wooden or metal frames by narrow strips of lead. As techniques improved and glass became less expensive, the panes increased in size and the original casement form was gradually modified. By 1850, it was possible to glaze window sashes in only one or two units, leading to the double-hung sash form in common use today.

During much of the Middle Ages in Europe, chimneys were not yet in common use. Smoke escaped from the building through small roof openings in the attic area. When chimneys were introduced, it became possible to floor second stories and attics for additional living space. In early American houses, chimneys were constructed of wood and clay (which represented a constant fire hazard) or, preferably, of stone, brick, or a composite of the two. Exterior placement was at the end (gable) wall or the side (eave) wall. The interior chimney was variously placed at the end, slope, or ridge of the roof.

The principal building material in the Northeast was wood, and early New

England dwellings were usually only one room deep and two stories high, built on an I-plan with a central chimney (later, with paired chimneys). Single-story hall-and-parlor dwellings modeled on their English predecessors were also constructed, with the same heavy timber framing covered with boards or shingles for weatherproofing.

Farther south, the colonists built single-story frame or masonry houses with the chimney at the gable end—a pattern that continued in the log cabins constructed by immigrants to the Middle Colonies from the heavily timbered areas of central and northern Europe, including Germany and Sweden.

As the original English colonies became more affluent, the English Georgian style gained wide acceptance for both housing and public buildings (1700-1776). This familiar style was based on classical design principles as interpreted by the influential Italian architect Andrea de Pietro, known as Palladio (after Pallas Athena, the Greek goddess of wisdom). In 1570 he had published the *Quattro Libri* (*Four Books on Architecture*), which had incalculable influence on European architects and formed the basis of a classical revival in England and, later, in North America.

In adapting antique forms to Renaissance buildings, Palladio erroneously assumed that ancient houses were fronted with great temple porticoes like those he had studied in Rome, and he incorporated one on each face of his famous Villa Capra, known as the Villa Rotunda, near Vicenza. The Roman Pantheon was his model for both the porticoes and the central dome. Two centuries later, the elegance of his designs and their practical advantages (including protection from the sun and ventilation) made them popular with wealthy plantation owners in the southern United States. The style was adapted for innumerable churches, schools, and government buildings in the expanding colonies. Georgian architecture is recognized by its balanced, symmetrical proportions, classical detailing, center-hall floor plan, and ornamental doorways, surmounted by pediments (later, fanlights) and often flanked by narrow windows called sidelights, or by pilasters—flattened columns projecting from the façade. Arched doors, windows, and porches of the segmental type are also characteristic of this style.

The earliest American town houses, with narrow front façades and linear plans, were widely built before the Revolutionary War in coastal cities, but few examples survive except in Boston, Philadelphia, and Alexandria, Virginia. In England, where the Georgian style flourished between 1650 and 1750, the principal architects were Inigo Jones, James Gibbs, and Sir Christopher Wren.

Below: Small glazed windows like this one below the roofline became increasingly common during the seventeenth century. At the same time, stone or brick chimneys were replacing the hazardous wood-and-clay chimneys, which needed constant repair to prevent hidden chimney fires.

The style came to the New World primarily through architectural manuals, or pattern books, which were widely used by Colonial artisans. In fact, most of our early Georgian landmarks were designed by architects whose names are unknown.

After 1750 dormers and decorative quoins (patterned masonry at wall angles) became common in the English colonies. On brick buildings, the separation between floors was marked by a change in the masonry pattern (belt course). Other developments included two-story pilasters, centered gables, and roof balustrades. Cupolas projecting above the roof were seen primarily on public buildings.

The Federal or Adam style developed from the Georgian and was established in America by wealthy New England merchants along lines laid out by the Adam brothers, England's most popular architects in the late eighteenth century. Robert Adam had traveled to Italy and other Mediterranean countries to study classical buildings first-hand, which led to a new interest in the classical monuments themselves, rather than as they had been interpreted since the early Renaissance. The Adam brothers also popularized such design elements as garlands, swags, and urns.

During this period, the first true American architects emerged. They included Charles Bulfinch, who was known primarily for his work in and around Boston; William Jay (Savannah, Georgia); Benjamin H. Latrobe (Philadelphia and Virginia); Samuel McIntire (Salem, Mass.); and A. Parris (Maine). Residents of the wealthy port cities were willing to pay for stylish houses that reflected their status; so were members of the new landed gentry. Many impressive Adam-style houses rose along the Eastern Seaboard, from Boston, Salem, and Marblehead, Massachusetts, to

Newport and Providence, Rhode Island; Philadelphia; New Castle, Delaware; New York City; Charleston; Savannah; and Georgetown, in the District of Columbia, where the U.S. Capitol building, designed by William Thornton (the first of a series of Capitol architects), was still under construction.

The symmetrical Adam-style house resembled the Georgian in that its doors and windows were arranged in ranks: they were never paired. However, the later style more frequently featured projecting wings and similarly styled dependencies or outbuildings. Adam door surrounds were even more elaborate than the Georgian, surmounted by semicircular or elliptical fanlights accompanied by sidelights, and often extended into a small entry porch. The cornice of the Adam house was emphasized by toothlike dentils or other decorative moldings, and windows were typically ranked in series of five along the two-story façade. Elaborations of the style might include roof-line balustrades; a Palladian-style window in the second story above the main entrance; and the use of flat or keystone lintels above the windows, with prominent sills below. Front stair rails of iron were often used, and sometimes iron balconies and curved front bays, especially in Boston.

Above: Restoration of the Governor's Palace (1720; addition, 1751) at Williamsburg, Va. Sir Christopher Wren is believed to have designed the original Georgian building, although he never came to the colonies. It was not uncommon for English architects to provide plans for important Colonial buildings. The addition architect was Robert Taliaferro.

Thomas Jefferson was a major influence on the Classic Revival style in post-Revolutionary America, in spite of the vociferous objections of patriots like Thomas Paine, who felt that the new nation should have its own new style. Jefferson's ongoing experiments at Monticello (from 1769) were based on Roman prototypes, as was his design for the University of Virginia (1825). Its focal point is the library, called the Rotunda, which was modeled on the Roman Pantheon. His other masterpiece is the State Capitol building at Richmond (1784), loosely adapted from the Roman Maison Carrée built at Nimes, France, about 16 BC. However, by the 1820s, the more strictly classical Greek Revival style was gaining ascendancy over the Federal style, a process that can be traced in the evolution of Monticello and that occurred even earlier in much of the South. Houses in the Greek Revival style usually have a wide band of trim beneath the eaves, recalling the entablature of Greek temples. Low-pitched roofs are the norm. Many have full-height entry porches with large columns, although some have neither. Houses built in this style are often

oriented so that the gable end becomes the front façade, reminiscent of Greek prototypes.

Following the Medieval- and Renaissance-inspired styles, the next American style based on historic precedents is the Neoclassical (1895-1940), usually interpreted as the two-story house with prominent columns the full height of the façade. These columns commonly have elaborate capitals based on either Greek or Roman models. Neoclassical buildings take various forms, and details characteristic of the Renaissance Classical movement often occur.

Dutch Colonial houses in the Middle Colonies, including New York, New Jersey, Delaware, and Pennsylania, showed the influence of Dutch, German, Swedish, and English architectural styles. The Dutch colonies soon passed into English hands, so the original style has been much diluted. The commonest construction material was brick (urban) or stone (rural areas). The shuttered windows were small-paned, roofs were side-gabled, and batten (vertical board) doors were the norm, frequently divided into two sections.

Right: This Georgian plantation house on the James River in Richmond, Va., has a hipped roof with dormers, more commonly seen in the Southern colonies than in the Northeast. The mansion reflects the influence of the Adam and Greek Revival styles in its symmetry, porch style, and window placement.

The earliest Dutch dwellings in America were of the postmedieval type, with steeply pitched parapeted roofs and paired end chimneys. For rural houses, coursed stone rather than brick was the usual material. The familiar gambrel (barn-shaped) roof became popular in the 1750s and is still a common sight in such areas as Long Island and Pennsylvania, as well as farther west. It was adopted for vernacular folk houses sometimes far removed from the original Dutch colonies.

French Colonial style dominated the architecture of the Midland region, comprising the original Illinois Country and the vast Louisiana Territory. The first French immigrants were primarily trappers and traders, who established few communities except for their stockades and trading posts. However, by 1700, permanent settlers were building houses reminiscent of their French prototypes; these were primarily single-story, with many narrow door and window openings flanked by paired shutters. Steeply pitched roofs were the norm; later, lower hipped roofs became increasingly common. Walls were usually of stucco over a half-timbered frame.

The French-style urban cottage survives in a few parts of New Orleans, although most remaining examples have been altered. The typical cottage had no porch but fronted directly on the adjacent sidewalk. The roof, usually side-gabled, had flaring eaves. In rural areas, French Colonial houses had extensive porches, usually supported by masonry columns over a high masonry foundation. Most had steeply pitched hipped roofs that dated back to the time when thatched roofs were built at a steep pitch to shed water more readily. In milder climates like that of Louisiana, the porch might extend around most of the house, like the bungalow style imported from

the Far East via the West Indies. When the roof was extended over such porches at a gentler pitch, the result was a distinctive dual-pitched form that persisted in some areas until the Civil War.

To summarize, the majority of styled houses in colonial and postcolonial America derived from three primary traditions: the Medieval, originating largely in England and France as the Gothic style; the Renaissance Classical interpretation of ancient models, as seen in the Georgian and Adam styles; and the inspiration derived more directly from ancient classical models, as seen in the Greek Revival and other Neoclassical forms. Other traditions that influenced colonial and later architecture included the Spanish, closely allied in North America with the indigenous pueblo style, and such lesser influences as the Oriental, Egyptian, and other so-called "Exotic" styles, which will be explored in a subsequent chapter. Most of these, in turn, were destined to be revived and reinterpreted over time. Their influence can be seen to the present day, especially among post-Modernist architects who turned away from the impersonality they preceived in twentieth-century Machine Age modernism to become more responsive to historic influences.

Above: *New England Colonial style dominates the campus of Dartmouth College in Hanover, N.H., founded in 1769 under a charter granted by King George III. Additions have been in keeping with the original classic style.*

The Wren Building, 1695 *Above*
This landmark building at the College of William
and Mary, Williamsburg, Va., may have been
designed by Sir Christopher Wren. The original
building burned in 1705, but was rebuilt. The
chapel wing was added in 1732.

Gunston Hall, 1758 *Opposite, above*
Sensitively restored, Gunston Hall, in Fairfax
County, Va., is an excellent example of the Georgian
style. Sir William Buckland designed the interiors.

The John Whipple House, 1640 *Opposite, below*
This postmedieval-style frame house with diamond-
paned casement windows is located in Ipswich,
Mass. It closely resembles the contemporaneous
John Turner House in Salem, Mass., made famous
by Nathaniel Hawthorne as "The House of the
Seven Gables."

The Lancaster Meeting House, 1817 *Right*
Also known as the First Church of Christ, Lancaster,
Mass., this building is often considered the master-
work of Charles Bulfinch, one of the first great
American-born architects.

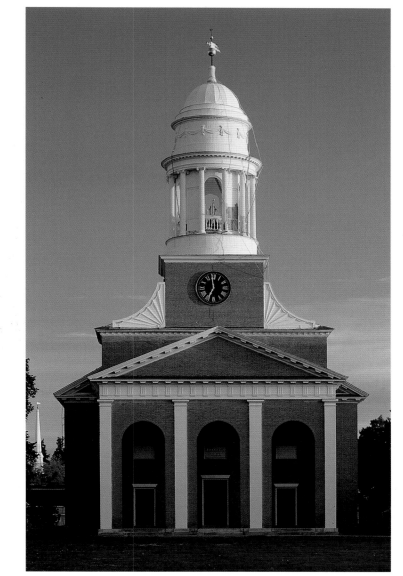

Governor John Langdon House, 1784 *Left*
This post-Revolutionary governor's mansion in Portsmouth, N.H., shows the restrained elegance and fine detailing of the late Georgian style. The double-hung sash windows are placed singly in symmetrical rows, and a graceful balustrade surmounts the entry porch.

John Brown House, 1788 *Right*
This Adam-style house in Providence, R.I., was designed by Joseph Brown and enlarged at a later date. The columned entry portico has a decorative cornice with balustrade above. A classic Palladian window is centered over the doorway.

The Moffit-Ladd House, 1764 *Below*
This elegant door surround has an unbroken triangular pediment and columns; the first-floor windows have segmental crowns and the second-floor windows are crowned by broken pediments. The architect of the colonial house, located in Portsmouth, N.H., is unknown.

Doorway Detail in the Adam Style *Below*
The fanlight over this Adam-style doorway in Newport, R.I., has a keystone in the arched surround, as does the larger fanlight in the pediment above. Fluted pilasters flank the paneled door.

The United States Capitol Building *Opposite*
The Capitol Building in Washington, D.C., was
designed by William Thornton in 1793. The roster
of American architects involved in its construction
and restoration over the years includes Benjamin
Henry Latrobe, Charles Bulfinch, Robert Mills, and
Thomas Ustick Walter.

The Massachusetts State House, 1798 *Below*
Charles Bulfinch designed Boston's elegant
Massachusetts State House, still considered one of
the nation's finest buildings. It has been added on to
several times, but the original rectangular design,
with its wooden portico and columns supported by
arches, has not been obscured. The great gilded
dome has been a landmark for two centuries.

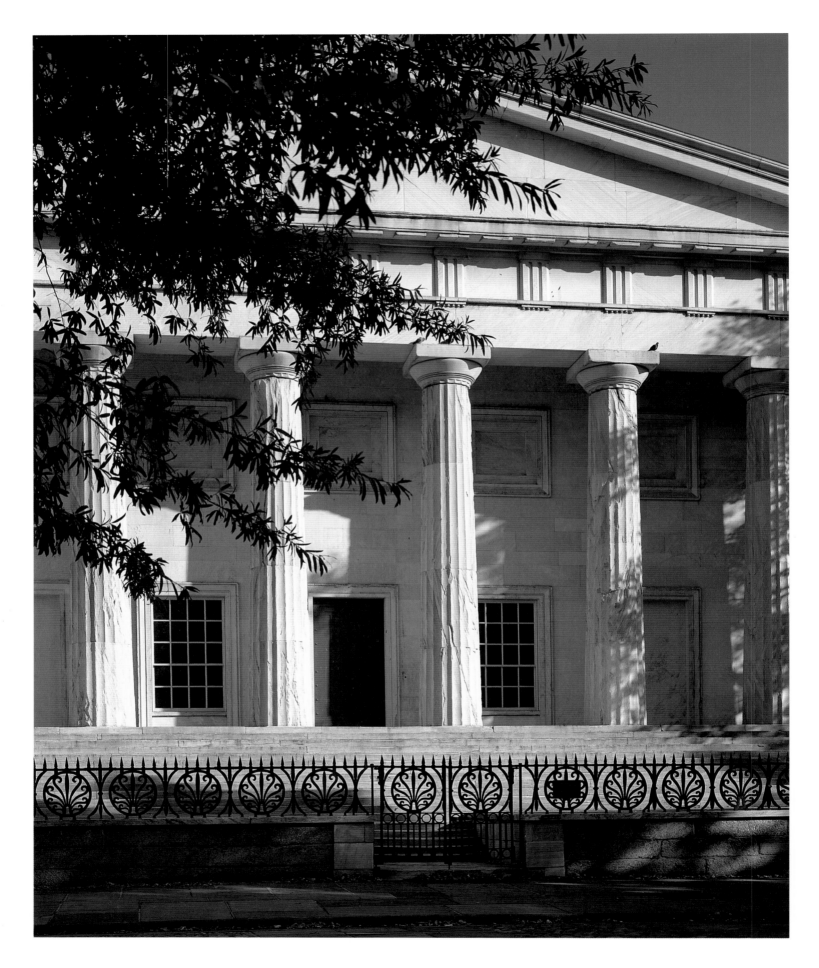

Mount Vernon, 1743 *Above*

George Washington's historic home overlooks the Potomac River in Fairfax County, Va. The original house was built by Washington's half-brother Lawrence and was added to over the years until the 8,000-acre-estate comprised almost twenty buildings. Washington added the columned portico after the Revolutionary War.

The Second Bank of the United States, 1824 *Opposite*

William Strickland's first major building, in Philadelphia, Pa., established him as a leader of the Classic Revival movement.

The University of Virginia (column detail), 1824 *Right*

The imposing university complex in Charlottesville was Thomas Jefferson's last major project, based on the Roman prototypes that governed his later work at Monticello. He considered the university's campus and buildings his most important contribution to architecture.

REGIONAL AND FRONTIER STYLES

Some of the most vigorous expressions of American architecture occur in the many regional styles that developed to meet the needs of a diverse, restless and inventive population. Drawing upon many ethnic and national traditions, settlers were quick to adopt new building ideas and materials and turn them to practical use. From the simplest wigwam-type shelters built by early New Englanders along Native American lines to the most elaborate Spanish Colonial cathedral in the baroque style, energy and imagination infused the architectural enterprise.

A case in point is the development and spread of the New England frame-house tradition from the early seventeenth century to about 1830, before the development of the railroad network that would connect the two coasts. The original area of settlement comprised coastal Massachusetts, Connecticut, and Rhode Island, where two-story houses of the hall-and-parlor type were constructed. However, the relatively greater confinement and severity of New England winters soon led to the addition of increased living space at the rear, which resulted in the one-and-one-half-room-deep saltbox and Cape Cod styles. As the affluence of the coastal settlements increased, larger frame houses two rooms deep became more common, and the traditional central chimney evolved into paired chimneys at either end of the roof. Central-hall plans came into greater use, and doorways began to be styled in the Georgian mode at an early date, before the Revolution.

In the early nineteenth century, the Greek Revival style made prominent front gables fashionable, and this style was exported, like its predecessors, into northern New England and as far west as the Great Lakes by about 1830. After completion of the transcontinental railroad, New England saltboxes were trans-

Right: An abandoned frame folk house in rural Mississippi. The walls are clad in weatherboard, and the interior chimneys are paired. Note the shedlike extension of the roof. Eventually, some kind of porch was added to most Southern houses to extend the living space outdoors.

planted as far west as Portland, Oregon, and Seattle, Washington, where they were surrounded by cottage gardens dating back to postmedieval England, the seeds of which had been painstakingly imported to—and eventually, across—the New World.

English colonists in the coastal South built the same types of folk houses as their Northern contemporaries, but the single-story form was commoner there, and brick masonry was established as an early alternative to frame construction. The milder climate made smaller dwellings possible, and kitchens and other outbuildings were often detached rather than connected. Between about 1700 and 1750, the single-room shelter with end chimney evolved into a larger hall-and-parlor-style house with an exterior chimney at each gable end. Affluent Southerners soon added stylistic details in the Georgian and later, Adam, styles, in both timber and masonry construction. By the late eighteenth century it had become common to extend living space outdoors in the form of the full-width, shed-roofed front porch which provided relief from the sun and the region's many seasonal thunderstorms.

Immigrants from Germany and Central Europe first built the log cabins that figure so prominently in American history and folklore. They settled primarily in the Middle Colonies of Pennsylvania, New Jersey, Delaware, and Maryland, and their houses ranged from simple, single-room plans with a single exterior chimney to the Continental log house comprising three rooms with a central chimney. This form, too, spread west with the pioneers who traversed the Appalachians to open the American heartland to European settlement. In the process, Scotch-Irish immigrants and a new wave of English colonists adopted the log-house plan, which became the characteristic form of the Midwest tradition until well into the 1800s.

Where additional space was required, the single-room log cabin evolved into a two-room plan with a separate front entrance to each room and a central chimney at the roof ridge-line. Sometimes the chimney remained at the gable end, outside the walls, with a second

Top and Above: *Two examples of the sod houses built by Great Plains settlers. The first—a dugout—was partially excavated, then walled and roofed with sod; both homes have timber framing for the doorway.*

chimney added at the opposite side. Another development was the two-room log house with dogtrot—a center passage often enclosed as a hall.

The difficulty of adding to the original massive log structure was addressed by frame extensions which might take the form of an ell; a shed-roofed single story comparable to that of the saltbox style; a side-by-side room with additional chimney, or a porch-cum-roof added to the front.

Many of the original log houses were eventually covered with weatherboards, as sawmills came to provide ready sources of precut lumber. Even then, the origi-

nal log form remained popular, and many examples have been preserved or restored. Second-generation log houses generally have larger gaps between the timbers, as they were designed to be weatherproofed by shingles or exterior boarding. The true log cabin (as opposed to log house) was commonly chinked with clay. Its timbers were left round and joined at the corners by overlapping saddle notches. The sturdier, more weatherproof, log house had walls of square-hewn logs closely joined by corner notching.

By the time Americans reached the Great Plains in the mid-nineteenth century, they faced a new set of challenges in building shelter. Here, wood was far less common and available (until the expansion of the western railroad network some decades later), so settlers improvised with crude masonry constructions modeled loosely on Native American models. Where thick soil covered rock that could have served as building stone, pioneers in Kansas, Nebraska, the Dakotas, and surrounding areas developed techniques of building with sod. Specially designed plows were used to cut the topsoil, with its tough plains-grass roots, into bricklike units that were used to build thick walls that gave protection from the region's bitter winters and sweltering summers. Often, these walls were erected over partial dugouts that were also roofed with sod. Frame extensions might be added over time, and some sod houses were two stories high. Stables and outbuildings were of similar construction. Brick was used primarily near transport centers served by rail or waterways, and all-timber construction was an expensive luxury.

As mentioned earlier, building styles in the arid Southwest were an amalgam of Native American and imported masonry techniques, which differed primarily in their roof treatments. Spanish

Colonial houses of the pitched-roof type, usually of side-gabled form, might have steeply pitched shingled roofs over timber framing. More commonly, they had low-pitched roofs with coverings of tile in half-cylinder shapes. The flat-roofed, parapeted type lacked traditional framing. Instead, heavy horizontal timbers were embedded in parapeted masonry walls to support a heavy roof of earth or mortar, drained by cylindrical rainspouts projecting through the parapet on one or several walls. The Los Angeles area developed an unusual form rarely seen today in which an almost flat (shedlike) roof with overhanging eaves was covered with tar. Some early colonial roofs were originally thatch-covered, but most surviving examples have been reroofed with shingles or metal.

From the 1830s, Anglo immigrants began to bring their own building traditions into the former Spanish territories, adding wooden decorative details, primarily in the Greek Revival style, and double-hung sash windows. Shingled roofs were introduced on pitched-roof forms, while formerly flat-roofed adobe houses were renovated by the addition of framed shingled roofs above the parapeted walls. Two-story variants with cantilevered second-story porches dominated the colonial capital of California, from which the name Monterey Style is derived. New Mexico, western Texas, and Arizona became known for the Territorial style: flat-roofed, single-story houses with a crown of fired brick, rather than adobe, along the parapet.

The elaborate Spanish Colonial *hacienda* had porches in the form of colonnaded arcades to provide sheltered passageways between rooms and access to the internal courtyard. More modest houses had porch roofs supported by hewn logs that might be capped by carved brackets. Anglo influence led to the use of wooden columns in the Greek Revival mode rather than the traditional roof supports of massive timber. Another result of Anglo settlement was the removal of the traditional rear porch to the front façade. Both the Pueblo Revival and the contemporary ranch style are successors to the Spanish Colonial tradition.

As Southern cities expanded in the late nineteenth century, what came to be called the shotgun house became increasingly popular. These narrow gable-front dwellings, only one room wide, were basically an urban form of the familiar

Left: Native American adobe houses had to be regularly resurfaced with mud to check erosion by rain and wind. Their walls were made of sun-dried mud built up in successive layers (puddled adobe). Some authorities believe it was the Spanish who introduced adobe-brick construction; others cite evidence for its use in pre-Columbian North America. Here, a Tesuque Pueblo woman maintains her courtyard walls.

colonial hall-and-parlor plan accommodated to narrow city lots. Some scholars feel they derive from West Indian influence, and have identified characteristics tracing them from Africa through Haiti to the Southeast. It is certain that these inexpensive urban houses were popular with former slaves who settled in Southern cities after the Civil War. They became even more widely disseminated with the growth of the Craftsman movement in the early twentieth century.

The Creole cottage form was brought to Louisiana by French Canadian (Cajun) immigrants familiar with long-span roof-framing techniques. Commonly two rooms deep, these side-gabled houses often have the front wall moved back to make an integral porch under the steep roofline. In New Orleans and adjacent areas, French Colonial urban cottages were built in Creole neighborhoods at least until the Civil War. Very few survive in their original form in the oldest part of the city, the Vieux Carré. The French influence is still unmistakable there, but it has been much altered since fires almost destroyed the district in 1788 and '91. While delicate wrought-iron balconies often fronted second-floor French doors in the old Creole houses, the extensive use of cast-iron full-façade balconies extended around the sides of the building was an innovation of the later nineteenth century.

The elegant Southern plantation house began in colonial Virginia and spread as far west as Mississippi before the Civil War. Some of the best-known examples, like Monticello and Mt. Vernon, started out as very small dwellings that were expanded and modified over decades by gentleman farmers with an interest in architecture and advice from the new professional class of architects. English-American architect Benjamin Henry Latrobe, a friend of Thomas Jefferson, was instrumental in setting the standard for the Southern estate house, which was first built primarily in the Georgian style. As a founder of the Classic Revival or Neoclassic movement in America, Latrobe's influence is seen from the final form of the altered Monticello to the grand homes of the Mississippi delta. His espousal of Greek rather than Roman models informed the work of two of his most important students and colleagues, Robert Mills and William Strickland, designer of Philadelphia's Second Bank of the United States (1824).

Gradually, the Greek Revival gained ascendance over the Roman form, for both public and private buildings on a grand scale. It persisted until the Civil War, and its influence continued well into the twentieth century. Standard details of the style were widely published, and carpenters as well as architects became well versed in classic orders, pediments, and porticoes. In practice, however, the Greek Revival buildings often incorporated Roman elements such as vaults and domes, as seen in Benjamin Latrobe's Bank of Pennsylvania (1801) in Philadelphia.

Below: The antebellum Greek Revival plantation house reflected the luxurious way of life among wealthy Southerners whose fortunes were built on cotton, tobacco, sugar, and other labor-intensive crops cultivated primarily by slaves. Most estate houses of the Deep South were modeled on classical prototypes that provided ample ventilation and protection from the sun.

Architect and engineer Robert Mills worked with James Hoban on the White House and designed many influential buildings in the Greek Revival style, including houses, churches, and federal projects, notably the National Portrait Gallery, formerly the U.S. Patent Office (1840), in Washington, D.C. His fireproof Records Building (1826), in his native Charleston, is an architectural landmark, combining simple, dignified classic form with engineering that used only noncombustible materials (brick, stucco, plaster, stone, copper, and iron) to guarantee the safety of the building's contents.

With virtual completion of the nationwide railroad network late in the nineteenth century, both styles and materials were more widely disseminated than ever before. Domestic and public architecture became increasingly eclectic, combining newly fashionable details with indigenous frontier or regional hallmarks in a distinctive and pleasing way. In Monroe County, Michigan, for example, the provincial style was remarkably persistent and adaptable throughout the later nineteenth century, a pattern that holds good in many other parts of the country as well. In this Midwestern community, it is exemplified in the two-story rectangular brick house with a front-facing gable, off-center entrance, rectangular sash windows surmounted by slightly arched window heads, and sometimes an ell with cross gable. Such houses are variously trimmed with Greek Revival pediments and frieze boards, Gothic arches, Italianate brackets, cupolas, "gingerbread" fretwork, bay windows, and porches, but their basic, underlying form remains the same.

Another development of the later nineteenth century was the importation of the English Arts and Crafts Movement to America, which had far-reaching implications for architecture and interior design. It inspired Frank Lloyd Wright in the early stages of his career, as seen in the Prairie House style, and Gustav Stickley, publisher of *Craftsman* magazine, which fostered the Mission style and the "bungalow"—a name loosely derived from the Far East, where the Hindi word means house. As built in India, this rural type of dwelling was generally a one-story structure with wide eaves. It had few rooms and a maximum of cross-drafts via high ceilings, large window and door openings, and verandas on all sides to shade the rooms from intense tropical light and heat. The form was readily adaptable for low-cost family housing, and the *Craftsman* magazine and movement popularized it through mail-order plans that were disseminated across the country. The style became especially popular in California, where it reached its most impressive form in the Japanese-influenced houses designed by Charles S. and Henry M. Greene in Pasadena in the early 1900s. These developments of the Early Modern movement are discussed more fully in chapter 5, while the romantic and sometimes flamboyant Victorian age is explored in the following chapter.

Below: Longwood (begun 1861) in Natchez, Miss., is the nation's largest octagonal house, now a museum. It was never finished as intended because its owner died during the Civil War. Architect Samuel Sloan showed the influence of the Exotic Revival in the large onion dome. The Eclectic mansion also reflects Italianate features in the portico and the cornice detailing.

Rural, Middle Atlantic Region *Above*
This Pennsylvania dairy barn, with outbuildings,
recalls German settlers of the Middle Colonies, mis-
takenly called the Pennsylvania Dutch from the
word *Deutsch*, meaning "German." Mennonite and
other immigrants from Central Europe built sturdy
wooden barns with gabled roofs on fieldstone foundations, well lighted by tall narrow windows.
Similar northern European farmhouse styles can be
seen in New England.

Cape Cod Style *Right*

The durable Cape Cod style has been popular for domestic architecture since New England colonial days. This contemporary example retains the symmetrical paired windows and dormers of its forebears, with a large central chimney and single-story wings.

Mystic Seaport, Conn. *Below*

New England vernacular architecture is preserved at Mystic Seaport, Conn., a nineteenth-century whaling port. Its shingled houses and clapboard stores are typical of the coastal communities of the period.

New England Congregational Church *Left*

The serene simplicity of this Congregational Church in Milton, Mass., is typical of the Northeastern colonies, where such churches were commonly built along the village green, the center of community life. Many fine examples have been preserved.

Colonial Boston *Below*

Architects like Charles Bulfinch helped make the port of Boston, Mass., founded in 1630, an urban center of commerce, beauty, and culture before the Revolutionary War.

Old Ship Meeting House, c. 1681 *Opposite*

This frame building in Hingham, Mass. (architect unknown), is the only seventeenth-century meeting house in the New England Colonial style still in existence. Many consider it one of the nation's finest buildings.

Town Houses *Opposite, above*

Some of the nation's earliest town houses have been preserved in Georgetown, Washington, D.C. The new capital was planned by French engineer Pierre Charles L'Enfant at the invitation of President George Washington (1791). Unfortunately, many of the early Northeastern town houses have been lost to urban renewal. Some examples are preserved in Boston, Philadelphia and New York City.

Colonial Williamsburg *Opposite, below*

Colonial houses at Williamsburg, Va., which was the state capital between 1699 and 1780. The restoration of what is now Colonial Williamsburg, financed by John D. Rockefeller, Jr., began in 1926 and now comprises 88 colonial buildings on 173 acres.

The Charleston Style *Above*

Historic Charleston, South Carolina, has a disinctive architectural style influenced by British colonists who came to the city by way of the West Indies late in the seventeenth century. High-ceilinged rooms and broad piazzas at each level are well adapted to the humid climate of this Southern port city. After the Revolutionary War, local architects including Gabriel Manigault designed many handsome buildings in the Adam style here.

Drayton Hall, S.C., 1742 *Above*
This classic Georgian mansion near Charleston, S.C.,
is in the high Palladian style (architect unknown).
The original plaster moldings and hand-carved
woodwork of the interior are intact, thanks to the
National Trust for Historic Preservation.

Oak Alley, La., 1839 *Above*

This Greek Revival plantation house near Baton Rouge, La., takes its name from the twenty-eight live oak trees, now almost three hundred years old, that line its approach. The Greek Revival style accompanied the Southern planters as they moved west from the Old South into Alabama, Mississippi, and Louisiana from the early 1830s until the Civil War.

Antebellum Elegance *Right*

Natchez, Miss., is a treasure trove of Classic Revival mansions like Stanton Hall (also pictured on page 30). Graceful Doric columns support the full-façade porch overlooking the landscaped grounds.

The Creole Influence *Above*

Elmscourt, with its segmental arches and lacy iron-work, imported from Italy, is an unusual example of the historic homes along the Natchez Trace. In 1810 it was a simple, square planter's house, but its second owners, the A. P. Merrills, added large wings, the Mediterranean grillework, and interior fretwork after 1830. Ulysses S. Grant was entertained here.

Cajun Country *Left*

The French rural cottage style is exemplified in this Nottaway, La., house, raised on a high stone foundation with slender columns supporting the full-width porch.

French and Victorian Ornamentation *Right and Below*
Natchez, Miss., was influenced by the French
Colonial syle in the years before the Louisiana
Purchase of 1803. At right, it is seen in the raised
porch and sloping side-gabled roofs. The gazebo
helps extend living space into the outdoors, a
feature common to Southern houses of many styles.
Unusually detailed and delicate spindlework
ornaments the facade of the Savannah town house
shown below. This style is variously referred to as
"gingerbread" or Eastlake detailing (after Charles
Eastlake, the English furniture designer who advocated somewhat similar design elements during
the later nineteenth century).

Midland Vernacular *Above*

Simple timber buildings have been preserved at New Harmony, Ind., a Utopian community founded in 1814 by German immigrants fleeing religious persecution in the kingdom of Württemberg. In 1825 the property was sold to Robert Owen, the wealthy social reformer and industrialist from Scotland, who continued the experiment in community living. New Harmony became a well-known educational and cultural center before the Civil War.

Midwestern Carpenter Gothic *Above and right*

The romantic ornamentation of the mid-1900s was derived primarily from builders' manuals freely interpreted by local craftsmen. Architectural reformer Andrew Jackson Downing was instrumental in popularizing the romantic Gothic style in such books as *The Architecture of Country Houses* (1850). In its introduction, he wrote that "when smiling lawns and tasteful cottages begin to embellish a country, we know that order and culture are established."

Southwestern Style Home *Below*

Southwestern vernacular architecture still hews closely to Spanish Colonial forms, as seen in this Tucson, Ariz., house, with its central patio, colonnaded arcade, flat tiled roof, and protruding roof timbers. The exposed roof timbers date from pre-Columbian pueblo construction, when stone tools were used to shape timber framing, resulting in unequal lengths.

Mission Church of San Francisco de Asis *Opposite, above*

Taos, N.M., is the site of this rugged pueblo-style structure (1813; later alterations) in keeping with ancient Taos Pueblo, which has been continuously occupied since several centuries before the Spanish incursion. The pueblo peoples were descended from the ancient cliff-dwelling Anasazi.

Contemporary Southwestern *Opposite, below*

Arizona's Pedregal complex, with its bold geometric forms accentuated by landscaping with spiky indigenous plants like the saguaro cactus and the yucca, is entirely at home in its desert setting.

Western Vernacular *Above and right*
A multigabled Western house, above, in Aspen,
Colo., with Stick-style detailing, shows the late nine-
teenth-century transition between the preceding
Gothic Revival and the emerging Queen Anne style.
Gothic and classical features are freely combined in
the Silver Plume, Colo., residence at right. The
Rocky Mountain States experienced an influx of set-
tlers in the wake of the 1849 Gold Rush and the
subsequent discovery of silver lodes in the region.

Mansions of the Prosperous West *Opposite*
The King William Historic Area in San Antonio,
Tex., has a number of Victorian mansions in the
Beaux Arts mode built by wealthy German merchant
settlers in the late nineteenth century. This one,
Norton House (c. 1890), is an unusual Italianate
house based on Renaissance models.

THE VICTORIAN ERA

Below: Lyndhurst (1842; addition, 1867), in Tarrytown, N.Y., is Alexander Jackson Davis's most important Gothic style house. It was designed for Philip R. Paulding and enlarged for George Merritt in 1867. Davis designed in several different styles and was in partnership with Ithiel Town between 1829 and 1835.

Prior to the 1830s, architectural styles in the United States varied widely on a regional basis. The colonial period saw the Georgian style in high favor along the Eastern Seaboard through most of the eighteenth century. After independence from England was achieved in 1776, the Greek Revival mode was espoused, partly because it was associated with democracy. The architecture of the Southwest, as we have seen, evolved under quite different influences. But as transportation and communication spread rapidly across the continent, and the westward population movement gained momentum, it became possible—and fashionable—to experiment with a number of different architectural styles at the same time across the country. This trend gained impetus with the publication of Andrew Jackson Downing's influential *Cottage Residences* (1842), the first popular pattern book of house styles. It presented full-façade drawings of several new fashions, including the Gothic Revival and the "Italianate" house, adopted from Italian Renaissance models.

Prosperous buyers and builders had more choices, while less affluent Americans adapted stylistic details or built along the same lines on a more modest scale. It became commonplace to find Greek, Gothic, and Italianate houses side-by-side on tree-lined neighborhood streets. Larger, more imposing houses of this kind rose in the countryside and suburban areas. Exotic buildings, based on Swiss chalets, Egyptian, and Oriental forms, added variety to the architectural scene, although they never enjoyed the popularity of the more conservative styles. Octagonal houses were advocated by Downing and other architects, and some attractive features of this form were adopted by later architects, including Frank Lloyd Wright in the early phases of his career. Thus, although there were many variations, the first national architectural style developed during the Victorian era, so called for the reign (1837–1901) of England's Queen Victoria.

The Gothic Revival had begun in England in the mid-eighteenth century, when Sir Horace Walpole remodeled his country estate in the medieval style, adding battlements and multiple pointed-arch windows, roof pinnacles, turrets, decorative tracery, and grouped chimneys. Other landowners followed his example, and the Gothic country house had been fashionable in England for almost a hundred years before the first fully developed example was built in the United States (Glen Ellen, in Baltimore, Maryland). Alexander Jackson Davis designed it in 1832, and five years later he published the nation's first house-plan book, *Rural Residences,* in which the Gothic style predominated. Prior to 1837, publications on domestic architecture had not contained three-dimensional views and floor plans.

Davis's friend and colleague A. J. Downing popularized Davis's ideas in *Cottage Residences* and *The Architecture of Country Houses* (1850). The full-fledged Gothic style was used primarily in rural settings, as well as for churches and universities in urban settings. The many gables, tall turrets, and wide porches made the style unsuitable for domestic architecture on narrow urban lots. However, Gothic door, window, and cornice detailing was used on more modest dwellings.

Gothic Revival houses were built in both wood-frame (called Carpenter Gothic) and masonry materials. The former were usually covered with horizontal cladding, but vertical board-and-batten siding was also used. The style was on the wane by the 1860s, but interest revived with the publications of the English critic John Ruskin, a founder of the Arts and Crafts movement, who advocated continental rather than English models. The inspiration he provided during the 1870s resulted in what has been called the High Victorian Gothic phase, seen principally in ecclesiastical and public buildings.

The characteristic features of the Italianate style, which flourished between 1840 and 1885, include: two- or three-story height, often with a square cupola or tower surmounting a low-pitched roof; wide eaves with decorative brackets supporting them; tall, narrow windows, usually arched or curved above, often ornamented with crowns of inverted U-shape. Many Italianate houses are square or rectangular, and windows along the façade are ranked in threes above the doorway, which is flanked by the first-floor windows. Some have centered front-facing gables, while others are L-shaped, with roofs that are cross-hipped or cross-gabled.

Italianate town houses typically have wide, projecting cornices with brackets and flat or low-pitched roofs invisible from the street side. Where the square towers identified with the Italian Villa occur, they may be centered on or alongside the front façade or at the adjoining wings of an L-shaped house. Most towers have narrow paired windows with arched tops and low-pitched hipped roofs, but steep mansard roofs are sometimes observed as well.

Italianate detailing is most prominent in windows, doorways, cornices, and porches. Most window sashes have one- or two-pane glazing, with arched and curved tops; sometimes the entire window is elaborately framed. Window crowns include hooded, bracketed, and/or pedimented forms and windows are often paired. Doorways are ornamented in the same styles, and paired doors are common.

Most Italianate houses have small entry porches or full-width porches supported by square posts with beveled corners. Large eave brackets along the cornice line are variously shaped and usually placed singly or in pairs.

The Italianate style was especially popular in the burgeoning towns and cities of the Midwest. Most of San Francisco's earliest town houses, too, were built in this style. It was least common in the South, where Civil War, Reconstruction, and depression curtailed new building while the style was at its height.

Exotic Victorian-age houses were inspired principally by Egyptian, Oriental, and Swiss Chalet models imported from Europe and the Far East by way of such influences as Napoleon's Egyptian campaign of the late 1700s. The rare Egyptian style is seen primarily in the form of massive fluted columns flared at the top. Alexander J. Davis designed the Egyptian-style Apthorp House in New Haven, Connecticut, in 1837, but subsequent additions have obscured its original cubical form.

The hallmarks of the Oriental style are ogee (S-curve) arches, both plain and elaborated, onion-shaped Turkish domes, and geometric patterns in masonry. Sometimes these details were imposed upon a typically Italianate cube-shaped form, creating an eclectic effect. Perhaps the best-known example in this style is Olana, the Hudson River Valley home designed by landscape painter Frederic E. Church in 1874 (architect, Calvert Vaux). Its fanciful towers, exotic archways, and multi-level roofline soon made it a landmark. Another "exotic" import to the American scene was Switzerland's traditional chalet, with its low-pitched, front-gabled roof and wide eave overhangs. Here, too, the romantic Andrew Jackson Downing was a moving force, recommending the form in his 1850 pattern book for "bold and mountainous" sites. It is readily recognized by the second-story porch or balcony with flat cut-out balustrade and trim. Patterned stickwork decoration on exterior walls is another feature. Alexander Jackson Davis designed one of the American prototypes, Montgomery Place near Barrytown, New York, in 1867.

The Octagon house (now rare) was a novelty in 1849, when lecturer Orson S. Fowler published a pattern book that espoused the style as providing more floor space and better light and ventilation than the conventional square house. The octagonal shape had been used occasionally on Adam-style houses for wings and projections, and Thomas Jefferson had experimented with it for his summer house,

Right: The J. M. Carson House (1887), Eureka, Calif. The Exotic Revival brought new romanticism to the Victorian house in the form of onion-shaped domes, here crowned by a finial, and other details that were freely combined with the Queen Anne style. Note the elaborate gable ornament in the Eastlake manner and the bay window in the tower. Low balustrades occur at ground and second-floor levels.

Poplar Forest (1819), but it was Fowler who popularized the style with his book *The Octagon House: A Home for All.* Some very attractive examples were built, especially in the Midwest. Undoubtedly, the exterior shape is pleasing, but considerable wasted space in the interior, where the floor plans were still rectangular, limited the style's popularity.

Another distinctive Victorian-age style was the Second Empire, imported from France by way of England during the reign of Napoleon III (1852–70). Its distinctive mansard roofline—dual-pitched hipped roof with dormer windows on the steep lower slope—makes it easy to recognize. Other features include molded cornices at top and bottom of the lower roof slope and decorative brackets below the eaves, as in the contemporaneous Italianate style. Façade openings are usually ranked in threes, and some examples have central cupolas or towers with mansard roofs and small dormer windows. The Second Empire style was popular for town houses in that it provided an upper floor behind the steep roofline that increased interior living space without becoming too massive for city lots. Larger houses could be of compound form—usually L-shaped—or have a centered wing or gable along the front wall with its own mansard roof.

Ornamental patterns of color or texture are often seen in Second Empire roofing material, and iron cresting above the upper cornices features frequently. Elaborate door and window surrounds with scrolls at the base, and paired windows within such surrounds, are typical and closely resemble those of the Italianate style. Entry doors are often paired, sometimes with glazing in the top half, and accessed by a shallow flight of steps. One- or two-story porches with balustrades above and below are another hallmark of the style.

Left: This Second Empire house has the characteristic mansard roof with dormer windows in decorative surrounds and cresting along the roof line. The single-story porch with balustrade above projects from the façade. Its arches replicate the shape of the windows and double doorway. A molded cornice with brackets bounds the lower roof slope.

The Second Empire style reached its zenith shortly after the Civil War. In fact, so many public buildings were constructed along these lines during the Grant administration (1869–77) that it was dubbed the General Grant style. Unlike the Greek Revival or Gothic styles, which were embraced in the early nineteenth-century partly for their romantic, picturesque qualities, the contemporary Second Empire style was considered extremely modern and up-to-date.

The Stick style came into vogue after the 1850 publication of A. J. Downing's *Architecture of Country Carpentry Made Easy* (1858). This picturesque, largely indigenous, style was transitional between the Gothic Revival and the Queen Anne: all three featured adaptations of medieval English building traditions.

In the Stick style, wall surfaces were a primary decorative element, patterned with horizontal, vertical, or diagonal boards called "stickwork." Sometimes all three patterns occur on the same building, along with decorative trusses in the gables and diagonal or curving porch support brackets. The common house form featured a steeply pitched gabled roof, overhanging eaves with exposed rafter ends or brackets, and wall cladding of shingles or boards alternating with the raised stickwork. Porches and bay windows are frequently seen, while the town house version has a flat rather than pitched roof. The latter are concentrated in San Francisco, where abundant lumber and a booming economy favored wooden house construction during the 1870s and 1880s. Richard Morris Hunt designed several elaborate "cottages" in this style in the Northeast, including the J. N. H. Griswold House (1862) in Newport, Rhode Island.

Closely related to both the Stick and Queen Anne styles is the Shingle style, popular for resort architecture during the late 1800s, especially in the Northeast: Newport, Cape Cod, eastern Long Island, and coastal Maine. An extremely diverse style, it is identified primarily by wall cladding and roofing designed to unite such disparate elements as irregular, steeply pitched rooflines; extensive wraparound porches; multilevel eaves; towers; dormers; and one- or two-story bay windows. Typical porch supports included plain or classical wooden columns, and sometimes shingled or stonework piers. Most of these houses were of asymmetrical, rambling form, and they were designed mainly by fashionable Eastern architects including Henry Hobson Richardson (whose Romanesque arches are a feature of the style), McKim, Mead & White, and John Calvin Stevens. On the West Coast, Willis Polk of San Francisco designed several notable examples. Frank Lloyd Wright worked in the Shingle style early in his career, and its influence is apparent in his home/studio in Oak Park, Illinois.

The Queen Anne style dominated domestic architecture throughout the late nineteenth century and continued into the early twentieth century. Examples are found across the nation, in varying degrees of exuberance, with a steady increase in dominance from the Midwest to California and deep into the South. The style was imported from England, where architect Richard Norman Shaw was its primary influence. The name Queen Anne is a misnomer, since her reign (1702–14) was characterized by a more formal Renaissance style. Shaw and his colleagues drew more heavily upon medieval models from the earlier Elizabethan and Jacobean periods in formulating the English version first seen here, mainly in half-timbered and patterned masonry forms. These were largely superseded by the indigenous spindlework adaptation, a process expedited by the availability of precut details, pattern books, and the nation's first architectural magazine, *The American Architect and Building News.* Perhaps half of the Queen Anne houses in the United States have graceful turned porch supports and spindlework ornamentation in the form of balustrades and/or friezes suspended from the porch ceiling. Such detailing is also seen in the form of roof cresting, finials, gable ornaments, and lacelike porch brackets.

The identifying structural features of the style include: steeply pitched roofs of irregular shape, usually with dominant, front-facing gables; patterned shingles; cutaway bay windows; and full-width single-story porches extending along one or both side walls. Decorative detailing used to avoid a smooth-walled appearance takes several forms, including half-timbering, bays, towers (usually placed at one corner of the front façade), overhangs, and wall projections. Where masonry rather than wood is the construction material, decorative stone and brick patterns, terracotta panels, and patterned chimneys are the norm.

Porch-support columns may be of the classical type, usually grouped in units of two or three. In such cases (called the free classic type), Palladian windows and cornice-line dentils are often seen. Town houses in the Queen Anne style are usually detached, rather than rowhouses, with front-gabled hipped roofs. Unfortunately, many of the finest examples, as in New York, Chicago, and Washington, D.C., have been lost to demolition.

Another interesting feature of the late nineteenth-century scene was the Richardsonian Romanesque style, adapted from European Romanesque models by the innovative Boston architect Henry Hobson Richardson. Trained at the École des Beaux Arts in Paris, he evolved his own personal style for major public buildings like Boston's Trinity Church and impressive masonry mansions that occur principally in affluent Northeastern cities. Features of the style include round-topped arches over entryways, windows, and porch supports; rough-faced, squared stonework; round towers with conical roofs; and asymmetrical façades. Some-

times, two or more materials in varying colors are used to create decorative wall patterns. Windows are usually recessed into the masonry walls, often paired or grouped in threes. Other forms of window elaboration include stone transoms and polychrome stonework lintels, while dormers are of the parapeted and gabled type, with some eyebrow dormers and other variations. Even in the 1890s, these houses were expensive to build, and those that remain are usually architect-designed landmarks.

What has been called the Folk Victorian style is broadly defined as Victorian-style detailing applied to simple one- and two-story houses of the type that were built all over the country during the nineteenth century. Such detailing includes porch spindlework; flat, jigsaw-cut trim; and cornice-line brackets in the Italianate or Queen Anne mode. However, Folk Victorian houses are identifiable by their symmetrical façades and by the absence of multi-textured wall surfaces characteristic of the true Queen Anne style.

Left: *This Folk Victorian town house shows Gothic influence in the gables at either end of the façade, with their stickwork ornamentation and finials. The unusual window treatment frames rectangular sash windows in an ornamental Syrian arch. Spindlework porch detailing across the symmetrical façade is another feature that distinguishes this as a folk house with Queen Anne detailing rather than a true asymmetrical example of the style.*

Prouty House, 1850s *Above*

This historic Gothic Cottage in Kalamazoo, Mi., is
dominated by its steeply pitched roof with elaborate
tracery at the gable ends and dormers. The hanging
bay window may have come from a popular builder's
manual of the period. Tasteful Gothic pillars support
a veranda that unifies the two façades. The owner
and his family worked the land of Michigan's
Monroe County.

Yale University, Gothic Revival *Right*
The soaring Harkness Tower and other buildings on
the New Haven, Conn., campus of the nation's third
oldest university are in the nineteenth-century
Gothic Revival style. James Gamble Rogers
designed many buildings on the 175-acre campus.

Lockwood-Mathews Mansion, 1869 *Below*
Gothic towers, arches, and cast-iron roof cresting
make the Lockwood-Mathews mansion, now a
museum, a landmark in coastal Norwalk, Conn.

Detailing in the Gothic Mode *Left and below*
Three examples of Victorian-era Carpenter Gothic ornamentation inspired by medieval prototypes. Windows, like those at left, often have small gabled roofs with decorated vergeboards cut from wood by scroll saws. Vertical thrust is accentuated by numerous finials. The flattened Gothic arches at top left and bottom right are details of the Prouty House on page 54.

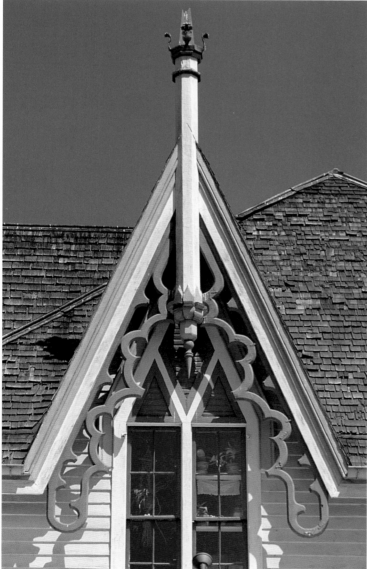

Victorian New Orleans *Right*
The closely related French and Italianate styles were popular in New Orleans, where narrow frontages are framed by ornate cast-iron fencing.

Midwestern Villa *Below*
The William J. Eichbauer House in Monroe, Michigan, exhibits many features of the two-story Venetian Villa mode of the Italianate style.

San Francisco Town House *Below, right*
This eclectic "painted lady" dates from 1890. It has been restored to its former glory and sensitively modernized.

Italianate Town House, Detroit *Opposite*
This elegant town house is a classic example of the towered Tuscan Villa Italianate mode, with molded cornice lines, triple windows, double doors, and delicate porch supports. The tower is unusual in having a mansard roof rather than the commoner flat or low-pitched hipped roof.

Suburban Tuscan Villa *Above*
An unusually fine example of the Tuscan Villa style in Monroe, Mi. The L-shaped house has a hipped-roof tower where the wing joins the principal section. Wide projecting eaves are supported by brackets, and the window crowns are of inverted U-shape.

Cape May, N.J. *Left*

Gothic and Italianate join hands in the McCreary House (1870), a delightful fretwork cottage on the New Jersey Shore, one of the nation's oldest and best-loved resort areas. Cape May is now a national historic district, and demolition no longer threatens its picturesque nineteenth-century houses.

Kennebunk, Me. *Below*

Italianate, Second Empire, and classical features combine in the Moody House, which is entirely at home in its setting: a former port, long since become a resort area, overlooking a snug harbor. The house was built in 1866, immediately after the Civil War.

Bank Building, Columbus, Ind. *Right*

The original Irwin's Bank (1881), a testimony to the growing prosperity of the Midwest in the 1880s, has elaborate bracketed cornices and window crowns of Italianate inspiration. It was renovated by architect Alexander Girard and now houses the Irwin-Sweeney-Miller Foundation.

Italianate Detailing, Midwestern Houses

Below left and right

The Italianate style was immensely popular in the Midwest and freely adapted to vernacular buildings of brick and wood-frame construction. The example at lower right is from the Allen Potter House in Kalamazoo, Mi. Heavy double brackets, dentilation at the eaves, and rope-turned pilasters at the front bay enhance the elegant entry porch.

Kamin House, Portland, Oreg. *Above*
This distinctive Second Empire house was built in
the burgeoning Northwest in 1871, when the style
was at its height. The dormers have arched window
surrounds, and single brackets ornament the
cornices. Quoins, a bay window with balustrade
above, and bracketed windows are attractive
features of the style.

Eclectic Victorian *Above*
This comfortable Romeo, Mi., house combines Gothic, Queen Anne, and Italianate features on an L-shaped frame house of the kind that was widely built in postfrontier Michigan.

Queen Anne Porches, 1890s *Right*
An unusually wide porch supported by slender columns increases the outdoor living space of a sizable Queen Anne house of the Gilded Age in the picture at top right. Delicate spindlework ornaments the raised porch on a Kalamazoo, Mi., home in the picture below.

Long Waterman House, San Diego *Above*
This handsome masonry house in the Richardsonian
Romanesque style was built in 1889. Its features
include a three-story tower with conical roof,
arched entryways, polychrome stonework, and
recessed windows. Note the eyebrow dormer in
the porch roof.

Queen Anne Adaptation, 1895 *Opposite, top left*
The Dorr French-Harold Allen House in Kalamazoo,
Mi., adopted the prevailing style to a narrow lot,
retaining the sweeping veranda and holding
ornamentation to a minimum. Note the beveled
corner tower with double-pitched roof.

Midwestern Folk Victorian, 1883 *Opposite, top right*
The builder embellished this L-shaped frame house
with Italianate moldings for a serene and simple
effect that is still fresh a hundred years later.

Suburban Queen Anne, 1890s *Opposite, below*
The asymmetrical façade is accentuated by the
extensive porch, rounded at the tower end of the
building. Door and window surrounds are simple,
and the cornice lines have delicate detailing. Queen
Anne was the dominant style in domestic
architecture from about 1880 until 1900.

High-Style Queen Anne *Above*

This unusually elaborated example has both stonework panels and shingle patterns to vary the wall texture. Decorative patterned chimneys, finials, gable ornaments, brackets, and spindlework are only part of the exuberant ornamentation.

Oak Hill, Marshall, Mi. *Left*

The eclectic Brewer House has a flat roof with cupola in the Venetian Villa manner and double brackets at the cornice line.

Pennsylvania Academy of Art, 1876 *Left*

Eclectic architect Frank Furness designed this highly ornamented Victorian building in Philadelphia, where most of his 600 projects were undertaken. Fortunately, it has been preserved intact. Furness studied with Richard Morris Hunt until the outbreak of the Civil War, when he enlisted in the Union cavalry while Hunt pursued his practice in New York City.

Kemper House, Indianapolis, In. *Right*

An elegant entryway surmounted by a Greek Revival-style broken pediment and dentilled cornices shows Renaissance detailing in the raised supporting columns.

Hackley House, Muskegon, Mi. *Above*
This is a fine example of the half-timbered Queen
Anne style, which is closely related to the Stick style.
Unusual ogee arches, belt courses, stucco patterning,
and decorative masonry chimneys add to the
impressive effect.

Trinity Church, Boston, 1877 *Opposite*
Henry Hobson Richardson designed this landmark
building in his own Romanesque style—the first
Eclectic style developed by an American and not
adapted from European revivals. His mastery of stone
masonry and wood gave his buildings a sculptural
quality widely admired by the public and by other
architects. A year before his death, in 1885, they
voted Trinity Church the best building in the nation.

CLASSICISM AND THE REVIVALS

The late nineteenth century was a period of increasing wealth and technology, built on railways, mines, steelyards, and high finance. Laissez-faire capitalism expressed itself in large, imposing buildings, lavishly decorated and appointed. Their forms and details were selected from a wide variety of styles from the past, often combined in a single structure. This Eclectic movement began before the Civil War, with the work of architects like Thomas Ustick Walter and John Haviland, as well as John Notman, who designed buildings in Gothic, Romanesque, Renaissance, Baroque, and other styles. The movement gained impetus after the Civil War and continued into the twentieth century, side by side with the Early Modern developments described in the following chapter.

New construction techniques evolved from the economical production of steel, which would replace cast-iron for multistory buildings; the introduction of efficient elevators; and machine-made tools and nails, widely distributed on the nation's railways. Balloon-frame construction, which had originated in Chicago during the 1830s, allowed cheaper and faster building with wood by using two-inch boards of varying widths joined only by nails, rather than hand-hewn wall timbers, painstakingly joined in post-and-girt fashion.

The Beaux Arts style that has come to be identified with the Gilded Age was popularized by American architects who had studied at France's École des Beaux-Arts, then the premier school of architecture. Richard Morris Hunt, its first American graduate, was prominent in bringing this style to the American scene,

along with H. H. Richardson, who would later take a new path. Based on classical forms elaborated by lavish ornamentation, the style is characterized by flat or low-pitched hipped roofs (sometimes mansard roofs); rusticated stonework (exaggerated joints) at the first-story level; masonry walls, usually of light-colored stone; decorative garlands, shields, and brackets on wall surfaces; arched windows with crowns; and paired columns or pilasters. Upper-story windows often have balustraded sills, and classical quoins appear on most examples.

Familiar Beaux Arts-style mansions by Hunt include Marble House (1892) and The Breakers (designed as a summer residence for Cornelius Vanderbilt, 1895), both in fashionable Newport, Rhode Island. The New York firm of McKim, Mead and White designed Rosecliff (1902), also at Newport, and many other East Coast mansions in the Beaux Arts style for wealthy clients. Mansard-roof examples, favored for urban houses, are found in Washington, D. C.,

Right: An art-glass peacock fills the skylight of a Romanesque rotunda — a style of ornamentation typical of Beaux Arts buildings of the late nineteenth century. This classical style, embellished by details of Renaissance inspiration, was advocated by American architects who had studied at France's École des Beaux Arts, beginning with Richard Morris Hunt. The term is also used to describe the entire period of elaborate Eclectic styles that prevailed between 1885 and 1920.

New York City, and a few other Eastern cities. Sometimes they are distinguished from the similar Neoclassical colonnaded style mainly by their elaborate façade decoration and the fact that they have paired rather than single columns, usually with Ionic or Corinthian capitals.

Beaux Arts architects included Nathan C. Wyeth, Henry Andersen, C. P. H. Gilbert, Charles Follen McKim, Paul Philippe Cret, Raymond Mathewson Hood, and Julia Morgan. The style remained a strong influence in American architecture even after 1915, when it began to decline, due partly to economic factors including the Depression of the 1930s. Its influence persisted in the form of planning the spatial relationships between buildings (an outgrowth of the École's enduring concern with composition, including balance and proportion). This was a primary force behind the City Beautiful movement at the turn of the century, which drew inspiration from the World's Columbian Exposition of 1893 in Chicago, for which Richard Morris Hunt had supervised the planning. Interest in formal design carried over to the emerging suburbs, with their parks and boulevards, and played a major role in urban planning for cities including Philadelphia, Cleveland, and Washington, D.C. Beaux Arts principles dominated architectural education in the United States until the 1930s, when Walter Adolf Gropius made Bauhaus tenets increasingly important in the formation of modern architects.

The Chateauesque style, which flourished between 1880 and 1910, was loosely based on the sixteenth-century chateaus of France, which combined Gothic elements with Renaissance detailing in masonry (usually stone) country houses. As built in the United States, primarily for wealthy clients, the style is readily recognized. Its features include:

Left: The Chateauesque style combined Gothic elements with Renaissance detailing in monumental masonry structures, primarily churches, public buildings, and great estate houses, commissioned by the industrial barons of the Gilded Age. In France, the revival of this sixteenth-century style, also called François I, was furthered by the influential École des Beaux Arts.

steeply pitched hipped roofs with many vertical elements, including spires, turrets, pinnacles, and decorative chimneys; multiple dormers, often extending through the cornice line, with steep parapeted gable roofs; and Gothic-style tracery or shallow relief carving at façade openings. The most complete example of the style is North Carolina's Biltmore estate, designed by Richard Morris Hunt for George W. Vanderbilt. Completed in 1895, it was landscaped by Frederick Law Olmsted, who designed New York City's Central Park, on a scale to rival its Loire Valley predecessors. Biltmore and its grounds are now a museum of period architecture and decorative arts.

Other embellishments of the Chateauesque style include conical "candlesnuffer" roof towers, finials crowning roof and gable tops, and arched doorways with Renaissance-inspired detail or ogee-arch molding. Canopies over doors are not uncommon. Balconies and towers often have corbeled brackets, and there are numerous balconies, both single and continuous. Dormer windows are often paired and occur both through and above the cornice line. Belt courses between floors may be single or doubled. Brick and smooth-faced stone are the commonest construction materials.

In the Midwest, architects Daniel Burnham and John Wellborn Root designed the Byram House (1880) in Chicago; other examples of the Chateauesque style were built in prosperous St. Louis, Milwaukee, and Cincinnati. Chateauesque town houses, both attached and detached, were built primarily in Northeastern cities during the 1880s and '90s.

In 1857 the influential Hunt had established an atelier, or studio, in conjunction with his office, and many young architects who were trained there in Beaux Arts principles became prominent designers in the Eclectic style. Among them were Hunt's sons Richard Howland and Joseph Howland Hunt. Others included Frank Furness, William

Robert Ware, and George Browne Post, who founded the nation's first school of architecture at the Massachusetts Institute of Technology, Cambridge, in 1868. Post designed the imposing New York Stock Exchange Building in Manhattan (1903) and a host of other public buildings in and around New York City, including Brooklyn's Old Borough Building (1897), the Long Island Historical Society Building (1878), and a master plan for what is now the City University of New York (1900–1907). Both his sons, William Stone and J. Otis Post, became architects and practiced with him in the firm George B. Post and Sons until his death in 1913.

John Russell Pope, a student of William Robert Ware, came to prominence as an Eclectic architect after he

Below: Detroit's F. J. Hecker House shows the unmistakable features of the Chateauesque style, including massive masonry construction, multiple towers with conical roofs, three-story bays, finials, and balustrades. Not surprisingly, the size and expense of this style precluded vernacular imitations.

attended the American Academy in Rome (cofounded by Charles Follen McKim) and the École des Beaux Arts. Born in 1874, he practiced from the late 1900s until his death in 1937, designing numerous churches, houses, museums (including New York City's Frick Museum), and public buildings, notably Washington, D.C.'s Constitution Hall (1930) and National Archives Building (1935). The National Gallery of Art and the Jefferson Memorial were completed after his death in 1941 and 1943, respectively. Two notable contemporaries of Pope were Cass Gilbert, designer of the U.S. Supreme Court Building (1935), and Paul Philippe Cret, the influential French-American architect and teacher whose reverence for Beaux-Arts design principles imbued his creations. His first American commission was the Pan American Union Building (1907), designed in association with Albert Kelsey in Washington, D.C. It is a classical Eclectic-style building with sensitive detailing and a graceful garden with a reflecting pool. The complex now houses the Organization of American States. Other notable Cret buildings include the Detroit Institute of Art (1922), Philadelphia's Rodin Museum (1928), and Washington's Folger Shakespeare Library (1929) and Federal Reserve Building (1935).

Another Eclectic building style of the period is the Tudor Revival, which draws upon various late-medieval English prototypes freely adapted to late nineteenth- and early twentieth-century buildings. The Tudor Revival style was first adopted for large, expensive houses in the burgeoning suburbs of New York, Chicago, and other major cities. Later, less expensive models became fashionable, and examples of the style are widely distributed across the country. Only the Colonial Revival style rivaled the Tudor in popularity during the 1920s and early '30s.

Stylistic features of Tudor Revival architecture include steeply pitched roofs, usually side-gabled; a façade dominated by a prominent cross gable; decorative (as opposed to structural) half-timbering; tall, narrow windows in groups, with multipane glazing; and large chimneys with decorative chimney pots. Most Tudor houses are masonry-clad, in stucco, brick, stone, or a combination of these materials. The early formal houses often have parapeted gables; others were roofed to resemble thatch-covered English cottages, with composition roofing materials layered heavily and rolled around the eaves.

Chimneys are usually very tall, with patterned brick- or stonework and round or octagonal chimney pots. Half-timbering is almost always confined to second stories and/or gables and occurs in a variety of patterns, which are usually infilled with stucco.

Doorway and window detailing on the Tudor house is often of Renaissance inspiration. Small cut stones (tabs) may project into brick door surrounds to give a quoinlike effect. Heavy board-and-batten doors are common, with round or Tudor arches (having flattened points) used in door surrounds and entry porches. Gables and second stories may overhang in the medieval fashion, and window styles include casements with cast-stone mullions and transoms, oriels, and one- and two-story bays. Decorated vergeboards are often seen on gables. "Strapwork" ornamentation, often of Celtic inspiration, may occur on high-style examples. More modest buildings are likely to have symmetrical façades: they started life as side-gabled folk houses and were converted into Tudors by the addition of a gabled entryway, a massive exterior chimney, and perhaps a side porch surmounted by battlements. These late examples of the style are often clad with wood rather than masonry and lack the typical half-timbering. Occasionally, one sees a flat-roof example with castellations all around, or shaped Flemish-style gables rather than the steeply pitched triangular form.

Masonry veneering techniques developed in the early 1900s contributed much to the popularity of the Tudor style, enabling builders to mimic the stone and brick exteriors of English prototypes at low cost. The style declined in favor during the late 1930s, although the Neoeclectic movement of the 1970s and '80s brought a modified Tudor Revival style back into fashion.

The Neoclassical style, which spanned the period between 1895 and 1950, was inspired primarily by the World's Columbian Exposition held in Chicago in 1893. A classical theme was chosen by the fair's planners, and prominent architects of the day designed imposing colonnaded buildings arranged around a central court. Smaller state pavilions established the precedents for Neo-

classical domestic design, which represented an eclectic fusion of four earlier styles: Georgian, Adam, Early Classical Revival, and Greek Revival.

Neoclassical buildings can be distinguished from the earlier styles in several ways. The façade is dominated by a full-height porch with a roof supported by classical columns with Ionic or Corinthian capitals. Doorways and windows often have a broken pediment above, although some examples have unbroken pediments, in the true Colonial manner. Windows are rectangular, with double-hung sashes, symmetrically arranged. They may have six to nine panes in one or both sashes, or be single-paned above and below.

Elaborations of the style include side and wing porches, roof-line balustrades, and full-width porches enclosed by low balustrades flanking the columned entryway. Triple windows of the Palladian type sometimes appear. After 1920 the original fluted columns with capitals gave way to slender unadorned columns, often square, supporting full-façade porches. The Neoclassical cottage was only one story high, usually with a hipped roof and a colonnaded porch. Sometimes the porch is covered by the main roof, sometimes by a separate flat or shed roof. Most Neoclassical houses have a boxed eave with a moderate overhang, often supported by dentils or modillions in the Adam and Greek Revival modes. Landmark buildings in the Neoclassical style are widely distributed across the country. They include the Willams House in Buffalo, New York (1895), designed by Stanford White, and the Governor's Mansion in Montgomery, Alabama (1907). Simpler versions of the style often have side-gabled rather than hipped roofs.

The Eclectic Colonial Revival style dominated domestic building in the

Below: A modest L-shaped Midwestern farmhouse of the mid-1800s was embellished by a spindlework porch later in the century. Similar improvements were made to many folk houses as prosperity increased after the Civil War.

United States from about 1880 through 1950. It expressed the rebirth of interest in early English, Dutch, Spanish, French, and other regional styles as freely interpreted in more modern idioms and materials. Mediterranean period houses included the Italian Renaissance, Mission, Spanish Eclectic, Monterey, and Pueblo Revival, while Eastern Seaboard models were the Georgian, Adam, and Dutch buildings of the Colonial era—the most influential phase of the style.

Pure copies of the originals are very rare: most examples combine details inspired by several precedents. Vernacular examples of wooden construction prevailed until about 1920, when improved masonry veneering techniques brought masonry houses back into favor.

Among the features that distinguish English Colonial Revival houses from Georgian and Adam originals are: paired, triple, or bay windows; single-story, flat-roofed side wings; broken pediments; and brick construction with Georgian doorways. Revival entrances sometimes include sidelights without a fanlight above, heavy elaboration copied from the English Georgian rather than the Colonial style, and pediments without supporting pilasters.

Dutch Colonial Revival houses, too, differ from their predecessors in several important respects. These include front-facing gambrel roofs with a projecting cross gambrel, steeply pitched gambrels with dormers comprising a second story, and a continuous dormer across the front, none of which occurs on original examples.

Much of the interest in colonial prototypes had resulted from the Philadelphia Centennial of 1876. The following year, architects McKim, Mead, White, and Bigelow toured New England and published their observations on original Georgian and Adam buildings. By 1886

they were building in the new style, which was refined by professional publications like *The American Architect and Building News.* Early examples were mainly asymmetrical in form, with colonial details superimposed, or symmetrical with hipped roofs, which was closer to the prototypes. Palladian windows were often used, and such features as broken pediments may be highly exaggerated.

After the Great Depression of the 1930s and World War II, the Colonial Revival style was simplified. Many examples of this latter form remain in use. They are often of the side-gabled type with restrained door surrounds and cornices, uncrowned rectangular windows, and modest overhangs (the Garrison Colonial type) with a brick first story and a wood-sided second story.

Among single-story Colonial Revival houses, the Cape Cod is the commonest form. Three-story buildings in this style include the President's House at Harvard University (1911), designed by G. Lowell; the Woodrow Wilson House (1915) in Washington, D.C.; The Midway town houses in Buffalo, New York (1890–1910), and numerous architect-designed rowhouses in New York City dating from the early 1900s.

Above: The Colonial Revival period that began about 1880 dominated residential architecture through the mid-twentieth century. Innumerable examples range from the single-story Cape Cod style pictured here to imposing three-story buildings, many of them loosely adapted from Georgian, Adam, and Dutch originals.

U.S. Supreme Court Building, 1935 *Opposite*

Cass Gilbert, an architect in the Beaux Arts tradition, designed Eclectic buildings in many styles derived from the past. The U.S. Supreme Court Building in Washington, D.C., is a particularly fine example. Gilbert practiced architecture for almost fifty years, and his designs are considered among the best of the late Eclectic period.

Neoclassical House, Madison, Ind. *Above*

A restrained example of the Neoclassical style that was popular between 1895 and 1950. The façade is dominated by a full-height porch supported by classical columns, and the windows are symmetrically balanced around a central doorway. The raised platform porch extends the full width of the façade.

Greek Revival Detailing *Above*

A front-facing pedimented gable and slender columns supporting the porch roof are among the attractive Greek Revival features of this late nineteenth-century Midwestern house. The Greek Revival became perhaps America's most widely accepted architectural style, and was adopted throughout the country for all types of building—domestic, commercial, and public.

The Breakers, Newport, R.I. *Above and Right*
Richard Morris Hunt modeled this seventy-room
"cottage" for Cornelius Vanderbilt on Renaissance
villas near Genoa and Turin. It was completed in
1895 at a cost of $7,000,000. The walls are of brick,
stone, and tile. Steel beams form a latticed network
that supports the vaulted arches of the interior, bear-
ing the weight of imported marbles, alabaster, and
mosaics. The detail at right shows the elaborate
Renaissance detailing of the colonnade.

Three Views Of Biltmore House, 1895

The Chateauesque Biltmore Estate is widely considered the greatest country house ever built in North America. Located in the Blue Ridge Mountains near Asheville, N.C., it was designed by Richard Morris Hunt for George W. Vanderbilt. Structurally, it is closer to perfection than the French Renaissance chateaux that inspired it. The park surrounding the estate originally comprised 125,000 acres, and the house itself contains four acres of floor space. The window detail at right is from the left side of the central tower.

The Pabst House, Milwaukee, Wi. *Above*

This Eclectic turn-of-the-century mansion has parapeted Gothic gables with triple windows and elaborate dormers extending through the cornice line.
Built in 1893 for brewery baron Frederick Pabst, it
is in the Flemish Renaissance style, with a tan
pressed-brick exterior decorated with carved stone
and terracotta. The interior was furnished entirely
from a seventeenth-century Bavarian castle.

The Glessner House, Chicago, 1886 *Above and Right*
One of Henry Hobson Richardson's few domestic
designs, this fortresslike house was designed around
an interior courtyard that admitted ample light to
the rooms. The floor plan was asymmetrical, open,
and expansive in a way that pointed to the new
direction of Modern architecture. During his brief
but brilliant career, Richardson, who died at the age
of forty-seven, a year before this house was completed, made a transition between the nineteenth and
twentieth centuries. The detail at right shows the
servants' entry to the house, whose austere beauty has
impressed other architects to the present day. Mies
van der Rohe visited it shortly after he came to
Chicago in 1939.

Pueblo Revival Style, 1910 – Present *Opposite and Above* Both examples illustrate the unmistakable features of this style, including flat roofs, projecting wooden roof beams, and earth-colored stucco walls. Some authorities believe, with justification, that Pueblo-Spanish Revival would be a more accurate term, since Spanish Colonial and Native American features are combined in this style, which is most prevalent in the Southwest. Building corners are generally blunted or rounded, and rough-hewn window lintels and porch supports carry out the hand-built look.

Tudor Revival Style *Above*

This turn-of-the-century building in Detroit, Mich., was from 1903 the home of Pewabic Pottery, one of the principal art pottery studios of the American Arts and Crafts movement, and is typical of the Tudor Revival style. Ornamental half-timbering, brick, and stucco form the wall cladding under a pitched roof crowned by a massive decorative chimney. Tall narrow casement windows in multiple groups, with multipane glazing, line the second-story façade, which overhangs the ground floor.

Post Office, New Ulm, Minn. *Opposite, above*

Medieval and Renaissance features combine in this atypical Tudor Revival-era building that reflects the community's Germanic heritage. Parapeted gables are lavishly ornamented, and tabs appear above and between windows for a quoinlike effect. Windows are grouped in lines of three at the ground-floor level and paired above. The arched doorway with pediment and pilasters is a Renaissance-style detail.

Dutch Colonial Revival *Right*
This example can be distinguished from the original
Dutch Colonial style by several features, including
the steeply pitched gambrel roof containing a full
second story and the dormer across the front, which
never occurs in originals.

Midwestern Vernacular *Above*
A young builder designed this Kalamazoo, Mich.,
house for his family in a composite style that
includes an unusual pagoda roofline and hooded double windows in the Italianate mode. Note the attractive detailing of the modest entry porch.

Beverly Hills City Hall *Above*

The Eclectic and imposing city hall in Beverly Hills reflects the burgeoning prosperity of Southern California in the early twentieth century. It is the centerpiece of a wealthy community that boasts luxury houses in every conceivable style. Nearby is the Mission-style Beverly Hills Hotel, a local landmark since 1911.

Eclectic Commercial Building, 1887 *Above*

The Cotton Exchange in Savannah, Ga, was designed by William Gibbons Preston. It reflects the growing importance of impressive commercial architecture in an era when cities vied for the tallest and most ornate "temples of commerce." Fortunately, this example has been preserved in Savannah's extensive historic district, the nation's largest urban area of its kind.

EARLY MODERN ARCHITECTURE

Below: Frank Lloyd Wright (1867–1959), a towering figure in the history of architecture whose career spanned seventy years. An artist whose most profound expression was architectural, Wright broke new ground with his imaginative, often daring, designs and experimented with myriad materials and methods of construction.

Modern American architecture is considered to have begun with the work of Louis Henri Sullivan, who was born in Boston in 1856 and entered the Massachusetts Institute of Technology at the age of sixteen. He remained at the institute for only a year, worked as draftsman in Philadelphia under Frank Furness, then moved to Chicago. There he worked briefly for the innovative architect William Le Baron Jenney, often described as the father of the Chicago School. In 1874 Sullivan left Jenney's office to study briefly at the École des Beaux Arts. When he returned to Chicago, where architecture was still booming as a result of the great fire that had almost destroyed the city in 1871, he joined the firm of Dankmar Adler, in which he became a full partner in 1881.

The fifteen-year partnership of Adler and Sullivan produced some of the most important buildings of the day. It also created the relationship between Sullivan and the young Frank Lloyd Wright that would have profound effects on both their careers. By the time Wright joined Adler and Sullivan in 1887, the young partners had become well known for tall buildings of cast-iron and steel that were restrained in style and refreshingly original in their ornamentation, which was based on a naturalistic decorative vocabulary in Sullivan's unique idiom. This stylistic direction became clear with his contributions to the Borden Block (1880) and the Chicago Joint Board (formerly Troescher) Building (1884).

In 1887 Adler and Sullivan received the commission for Chicago's Auditorium Building, an ambitious complex containing a hotel, an office building, and an auditorium with a capacity of 4,200 people. Their success with this landmark design, completed in 1890, put Adler and Sullivan among the top rank of Chicago architects, with Daniel H. Burnham and his partner John Wellborn Root, and William Holabird and Martin Roche, who practiced together in Chicago for forty years. All of them had worked with Jenney and were deeply involved in the evolution of functional design for tall skeleton-framed buildings.

During Wright's tenure with the firm, Adler and Sullivan produced the Wainwright Building in St. Louis and the Garrick Theater in Chicago's Schiller Building (both 1892). Wright worked

with Sullivan on the great Neo-Romanesque Golden Door for the Transportation Building at the influential World's Columbian Exposition in 1893. He was also instrumental in the design of the handsome Charnley House of 1891, which was richly endowed with the burnished woodwork, art glass panels, and spacious living areas that would characterize his residential architecture for years to come.

In 1893 Sullivan and Wright quarreled over Wright's undertaking private commissions for houses, and Wright left to set up his own practice in nearby Oak Park, where he built his home/studio. Adler and Sullivan continued their partnership until 1895, the year they designed the Guaranty (now Prudential) Building in Buffalo, New York.

During the five-year period that followed, working on his own, Sullivan designed one of the prototype Modern buildings: the Carson, Pirie, Scott Department Store (1904) in Chicago. The steel frame of the building was integral to the design, consistent with Sullivan's dictum that form follows function. This philosophy was expanded upon in his book *Autobiography of An Idea* (1924), which has influenced architecture to the present day. His later works included an impressive series of small Midwestern banks, notably the Security (formerly National Farmers') Bank (1908) in Owatonna, Minnesota, and the People's Savings and Loan Association (1917) in Sidney, Ohio.

Like his mentor Sullivan, Wright, born in 1867, had little formal training as an architect. He studied civil engineering for several years at the University of Wisconsin, Madison, not far from his birthplace in Richland Center, Wisconsin. Influences on his early work included Japanese and pre-Columbian art; the contemporary Arts and Crafts movement, with its emphasis on "honest" materials and workmanship; and the Victorian Shingle style, which he learned in the office of James Lyman Silsbee before he joined Adler and Sullivan. Some of these stylistic threads run through his impressive Oak Park home and studio, which he added to and altered from 1889 until 1909, when he left his wife, Catherine Lee Tobin, and

Left: Louis Sullivan's Carson, Pirie, Scott Department Store (1904) is regarded as one of the masterpieces of Modern architecture because of the clarity of its form and the richness of its ornament (see detail on page 100). The store, called Schlesinger and Mayer when Sullivan executed the commission, is of the powerful Chicago School loft type, rising from a delicate enclosure of cast-iron detailing at street level.

Left: Sullivan's inimitable ornamentation graces the Security (formerly National Farmers') Bank in Owatonna, Minn. (1908). His brilliance was not fully recognized until after his death in 1924, when he was acclaimed the first great Modern American architect. The Chicago School was widely admired by European architects and extremely influential on the Continent.

Above: The William G. Fricke House (1901), designed by Frank Lloyd Wright, is one of his tallest buildings in Oak Park, Ill., where he lived and worked from the late 1880s until 1909. This impressive forerunner of the Prairie House is Cubist in inspiration, reflecting Wright's determination to disassemble the traditional boxlike house and reassemble it in new ways compatible with human needs and modern technology.

their family of six children to live in Europe with the wife of one of his clients, Mamah Borthwick Cheney.

During his years in Oak Park, he designed numerous impressive houses in Chicago and its suburbs, gradually developing his Prairie style, which would have a profound influence at home and abroad. Wright's buildings were characterized by clean, clearly accented lines and interior spaces that flowed into one another, the structure rising from its site as an organic whole. He experimented boldly with new construction techniques and materials like the poured concrete used for Oak Park's Unity Temple (1906) and the pioneering glass-roofed office design for Buffalo's Larkin Building (1904). His masterful use of ornamentation combined the Arts and Crafts ethos with full utilization of machine-made products of high quality. Chicago's Robie House (1909) is a masterpiece of the Prairie style, which influenced other architects including George W. Maher, Walter Burley Briffin, F. Barry Byrne, George G. Elmslie, and William G. Purcell.

Houses built by Wright and the so-called Prairie School are identified by low-pitched hipped roofs with widely overhanging eaves; single-story wings or porches; eaves, cornices, and façade details usually in the floral or geometric Sullivanesque style; belt courses between floors; casement windows of leaded glass; pedestal urns; and broad, flat chimneys. Porch supports are generally in the form of square or rectangular piers. This style—one of the few indigenous to the United States—flourished between 1900 and 1920 all over the country initially in the Midwest. Eventually, it was spread by way of pattern books and popular magazines like *The Ladies' Home Journal.*

After he returned from Europe in 1910, Wright settled on his family property in Spring Green, Wisconsin, where he built, and rebuilt, the country house he called Taliesin. There he embarked upon a new phase of his career—a career that would total almost seventy years before it ended with his death in 1959. The intervening period saw new styles,

including the concrete-block houses of the 1920s in southern California, which showed the influence of pre-Columbian architecture, and the versatile Usonian houses of the 1930 and '40s—designed as moderately priced, single-story family homes with wood, glass, and brick elements under a slab roof. Wright's mature period is described at greater length in the following chapter.

Many designers who were part of the English Arts and Crafts movement, from William Morris onward, were troubled by the gap between their ideal of a humane and livable environment for the average family and the fact that their carefully crafted products were effectively limited to the wealthy. In the United States, the social component of the Arts and Crafts ethos was less pronounced. There was enthusiastic acceptance of well-made handcrafted articles for daily use, but they were, on the whole, more affordable than their English counterparts.

Several Utopian-style Arts and Crafts communities were, in fact, established in the United States, including Roycroft, in East Aurora, New York, and Rose Valley, New York, along lines laid down in England by John Ruskin and C. R. Ashbee in the mid-1800s. Here, workers lived together, earning modest wages for their furniture, book-binding, and metalwork. Simple lines and natural materials were the hallmark of the American Arts and Crafts style, but it did not achieve wide popularity until several American architects and designers took a hand.

Prominent among then was Gustav Stickley, trained as an architect, who founded his Craftsman furniture plant in Syracuse, New York, in 1898. Stickley had been impressed by C. R. Ashbee and other founders of the movement whom he had met in Europe, but his commitment was fueled by initiative and ingenuity in the true American tradition. His design magazine, *The Craftsman,* reached a wide audience, carrying mail-order plans for low-cost bungalow-style houses (called "Craftsman Homes") and advertisements for his plain Mission-style furniture, made of solid oak finished and stained by hand.

Other turn-of-the-century magazines embraced the idea of promoting hand-

Left: Wright's John Storer House (1924), in Los Angeles, Calif., is an impressive example of what he called his textile-block construction method. It employs three types of concrete blocks—plain, patterned, and pierced—in a two-story house with a flat roof and two wings.

Below: Wright's Wisconsin country house and studio, Taliesin East (1911–59), in Spring Green, was built of native materials including fieldstone and timber, with low cedar-shingled roofs. Over the years, it became a large complex whose fluid lines conformed to its hillside site. Many aspiring architects worked and studied here—and helped Wright with construction and miscellaneous chores.

Below: The Art Deco style was imported from Europe during the 1920s, a period of expanding wealth and travel. It is seen here in a 1930s example built in Albuquerque, N. Mex., with smooth wall surfaces and stylized decorative motifs along the façade (the cinema's marquee was added later). In some examples, surface ornamentation was reduced or eliminated altogether, as in the contemporaneous International style.

some, affordable housing for the average American. One of the most influential was *The Ladies' Home Journal,* which brought Frank Lloyd Wright to national attention in 1901 when it published his design for "A Home in a Prairie Town." This prototype Prairie House could be built for $7,000 from plans sold to *Journal* readers at five dollars per set. In 1907 Wright provided a plan for a fireproof, partly prefabricated house that showed his abiding concern with livable moderate-cost housing. Edward Bok, the editor of the *Journal,* had a house designed by Rose Valley architect William Price and was a tireless supporter of Arts and Crafts ideas.

Even established, fashionable architects like Ralph Adams Cram and Bertram Grosvenor Goodhue championed the movement. They were outstanding exponents of the Gothic style as "rediscovered" by John Ruskin. In

1908 they helped found the Boston Society of Arts and Crafts, and Goodhue designed several impressive Spanish Colonial Revival buildings for the Panama-California Exposition of 1915 in San Diego. His California Building, on the exposition site in Balboa Park, is now the Museum of Man.

Another Early Modern architect who studied with Louis Sullivan was Irving John Gill, born in 1870. His first designs were Eclectic, but he was soon experimenting with new building materials and methods. Like Wright, he focused on integrating buildings with their settings. Low-cost, hygienic housing was one of his primary concerns, as seen in the Lewis Courts design of 1910 in Sierra Madre, California. He had resettled in California for his health in 1892, and most of his mature work followed Southwestern vernacular forms, with details simplified almost

to abstraction. His experiments with tilt-slab concrete construction resulted in the 1912 Banning House in Los Angeles and the Women's Club in La Jolla (1913). Other notable buildings by Gill include the Scripps Institution for Oceanography Building, also in La Jolla (1908), and the Christian Science Church and Bishop's Day School, both constructed in San Diego in 1909. Unfortunately, his landmark concrete house for Walter Luther Dodge (1916) has been demolished.

Gill's concern with good craftsmanship was shared by the Greene brothers, Charles Sumner and Henry Mather, who practiced architecture in Pasadena, California, as Greene and Greene, from 1893 to 1914. They were among the most influential proponents of the domestic Arts and Crafts movement and their work made a lasting impression on Modern architecture.

Born in Cincinnati, Ohio, Charles in 1868 and Henry in 1870, they moved later to St. Louis, Missouri, where they attended a progressive high school sponsored by Washington University. There they learned to handcraft wood, metal, and other materials and became particularly interested in Japanese domestic architecture. After graduating from the Massachusetts Institute of technology, they established their practice in Pasadena and initially built eclectic houses that reflected their Beaux Arts-style classical training. However, within ten years they had begun to design simple Craftsman-type bungalows, which soon evolved in their hands into an intricately detailed style. Ideally suited to the California climate, these houses had an open Japanese feeling, with numerous low-pitched gables, open porches, and exposed wooden structural elements. Redwood and mahogany were used

Below: Cincinnati's Union Terminal, built in the Art Deco style in 1933 (architects, Fellheimer and Wagner), has been converted to use as a cultural center, in keeping with the contemporary movement for renovation and adaptive use of historic public buildings.

Right: New York City's Empire State Building (1931), designed by Shreve, Lamb & Harmon, was the world's tallest building when it was completed. The stepped-back upper stories and soaring vertical spire are hallmarks of the Art Deco style.

extensively—redwood for the exteriors and other exotic woods for the interior furnishings and fixtures. The Greenes' style is exemplified in the house built for David B. Gamble in 1908, now beautifully preserved by the citizens of Pasadena, with its landscaping and interior designed entirely by the Greenes. The total environment they created included furniture, carpets, lighting fixtures, and linens, and the wood-joinery craftsmen were closely supervised by Charles Greene.

Another impressive "ultimate bungalow," as the Greenes' high-style houses were called, is the R. R. Blacker house (1907), also located in Pasadena. Other notable examples include the William R. Thorsen House, built in Berkeley in 1908, and the Pratt House, in Ojai (1909). Their work was in great demand throughout the 1910s: it is believed that they designed some 540 houses in the Pasadena area alone.

It is unfortunate that the Bungalow style deteriorated over the next twenty years, largely as a result of poor copies that sprang up all over the country in the wake of publicity in the popular magazines. Pattern books not only offered plans for Craftsman-style bungalows, but precut lumber and detailing to be assembled on site. As a result, the one-story Craftsman house became the most popular in the nation for several decades. It appeared in various forms, including front-gabled, cross-gabled, and side-gabled, usually with partial-width front porches supported by square columns. Where beams or braces appear under the gables, they are not true structural elements but mere decoration.

Other popular houses of the early to mid-twentieth century include the ranch style, loosely adapted form Western frontier prototypes, and the Modernistic. In domestic architecture this style was called

Art Moderne; in commercial and public buildings, Art Deco. The latter style originated in Europe and received its first publicity in the United States in 1922, when the young Finnish architect Eliel Saarinen submitted an Art Deco design in the international competition sponsored by the Chicago *Tribune* for a new headquarters building. His design took the second prize and was widely admired by American architects, who felt he should have won. Publicity did the rest, resulting in many Art Deco apartment houses and commercial buildings during the late 1920s and early '30s: New York City's Chrysler Building is a well-known example. It combines the newly fashionable streamlined look with the vertical zigzagged forms patterned with decorative motifs that identify Art Deco. Very few houses were constructed along these lines. In residential architecture, Art Moderne, influenced by the streamlined look of new trains, cars, and planes, prevailed from 1920 to about 1940. These houses had smooth, often stucco, wall surfaces; flat roofs with a small ledge, or coping, at the roofline; and horizontal grooves or lines in walls and horizontal balustrades. Building corners might be curved, and glass blocks often figured in windows and walls. In later decades, the Art Deco and Art Moderne styles were highly influential during the development of the popular resort of Miami Beach.

When Eliel Saarinen submitted his design for the Chicago Tribune Tower in 1922, he was already an established European architect. His reputation continued to grow after he emigrated to the United States in 1923 and established his influential school of art and design at the Cranbrook Academy of Art, in Bloomfield Hills, Michigan. This elegant complex includes the Kingswood School for Girls (1929), the Cranbrook School for Boys (1930), and the Academy, with its reflecting pool (sculpture by Carl Miller). Saarinen's objective was to create an institution where all the design arts were integrated and taught together, and many talented young people were attracted there. He also practiced architecture with his son Eero (from 1937) in the well-known partnership Saarinen & Saarinen, which produced such notable buildings as the Kleinhaus Music Hall in Buffalo, New York (1938), and the Crow Island School in Winnetka, Illinois (1939). After his father's death in 1950, Eero Saarinen completed the commission for the huge General Motors Technical Center in Warren, Michigan, in association with Smith, Hinchman and Grylls (1957). He also designed the Kresge Auditorium and Chapel at the Massachusetts Institute of Technology (1955) and the Gateway Arch for St. Louis, Missouri, which was not completed until 1965, four years after his death. The Saarinens were among the most influential of the architect-émigrés who brought their abilities to the United States in the early twentieth century. Others included Austrian Richard Joseph Neutra, German Alfred Kahn, and the innovative founders of the International Style, whose work is described in the following chapter.

Below: Finnish architect Eliel Saarinen, who emigrated to the United States during the 1920s, practiced architecture with his son Eero Saarinen, who also had a profound influence on the evolution of Modern architecture. Eero Saarinen designed the Kresge Auditorium and Chapel (1955) at the Massachusetts Institute of Technology, Cambridge, site of the nation's first school of architecture.

The Monadnock Building *Below*
John Wellborn Root designed this restrained, all-masonry Chicago office building with its protruding bays. It was completed in 1891, and the south section was added by Holabird and Roche in 1893. Developer John Aldis (with Peter Brooks) praised the building's "Egyptian-like effects."

The Wainwright Building, Louis Sullivan *Opposite*
This St. Louis, Mo., landmark was commissioned to Adler and Sullivan in 1890 and completed the following year. It is considered one of the firm's masterpieces—the first tall building to be designed so that its steel skeleton frame is expressed in the exterior appearance. The ornamentation is unmistakably Sullivanesque.

The Rookery, Chicago, 1888 *Above*
Designed by the influential Chicago School architects Burnham and Root, the Rookery was widely admired for its graceful lines and elegant ornament. It was one of the first buildings to make use of a large light court in the center. The gridwork of the atrium ceiling was echoed in fluid cast-iron balustrades, lighting fixtures, and a curving oriel staircase. The building took its name from the old City Hall on this site, a gathering place for Chicago's pigeons and politicians.

Cast-Iron Façade, St. Louis *Left*
St. Louis, Mo., long known as the Gateway to the West, was among the first cities (with Chicago) to develop commercial buildings in the emerging Modern idiom, using cast-iron and steel framing with wide expanses of glass. Sullivan believed that a skyscraper should be "every inch a proud and soaring thing…a unit without a single dissenting line."

The Flatiron Building, New York City *Opposite*
Designed by architect Daniel H. Burnham (1902), the former Fuller Building derives its name from its unmistakable silhouette, a function of the narrow triangular lot on which it stands.

Detail, Carson, Pirie Scott Building *Right*
Louis Sullivan was unrivaled in the design of complex floral and circular geometric ornament in the style that graces the famous Chicago department store pictured on page 91.

National Farmers' Bank, 1908 *Above*

One of Louis Sullivan's later works was this landmark bank in Owatonna, Minn., which is especially
noteworthy for its great central arched window and
mosaic-like ornamentation in both the geometric
and floral modes.

People's Savings and Loan Association, 1917 *Right*

The ornamentation shown in this detail of Sullivan's
acclaimed bank in Sidney, Ohio, is a development of
the decorative themes displayed in the National
Farmers' Bank.

The Woolworth Building, New York City *Opposite*

Cass Gilbert's Eclectic Woolworth Building (1913)
was the world's tallest building when it was constructed before the First World War.

Frank Lloyd Wright Home And Studio *Above*
This was the Wright family home, to which he
added his studio, for twenty years. It was an evolving
demonstration of his fertile imagination and the
many influences that shaped his career, from the
Shingle style to Louis Sullivan.

Unity Temple, Oak Park, Ill., 1904 *Below*

In his text for the Wasmuth portfolio of his early works (1910), Wright described his first ecclesiastical commission as "a concrete monolith cast in wooden forms. After removal of forms, exterior surfaces washed clean to expose the small gravel aggregate, the finished result not unlike a coarse granite."

Interior, Unity Temple *Above*

Wright's unique mastery of space and light are apparent in Unity Temple, where weight-bearing volumes are cleanly defined in space etched out by the slender wooden uprights and horizontal moldings. The church was lighted from above by bands of windows below the coffered glass ceiling. Lighting and other fixtures were all of Wright's design.

The Robie House, Chicago, 1906, *Above*

The best known of all Wright's houses in the Prairie style is the Frederick C. Robie House, built on a narrow corner lot. It extends along a single horizontal axis, the most arresting feature being the cantilevered roof, which extends twenty feet beyond the masonry supports.

Meyer May House, 1908 *Left*

The warm and inviting interior of this outstanding Prairie House in Grand Rapids, Mich., shows Wright as a master of the principles he had practiced for twenty years. The dining room, seen here, is a study in burnished woodwork, patterned textiles, art-glass lighting fixtures, and clean uncluttered lines. The hollyhock mural at left is the work of artist George Niedecken, who often collaborated on Wright's interiors.

Window, Meyer May House *Opposite*

Wright's artistry is unmistakable in this view of the window treatment in the Meyer May House.

David B. Gamble House, Pasadena *Opposite top*
Perhaps the best-known example of Greene and
Greene's style is the Japanese-influenced bungalow
designed for David H. Gamble in 1908. The house
radiates out on several different levels under its low-
pitched, multigabled roofline, closely wedded to its
site.

Gamble House Interior *Opposite bottom*
The Greenes' dedication to craftsmanship enhances
every detail of the rich redwood and mahogany pan-
eling and wood joinery in the Gamble House. Like
Frank Lloyd Wright, the brothers designed interior
fixtures and furnishings in keeping with their buildings to create a total environment.

Irving John Gill, Women's Club, 1913 *Above*
After moving to California for his health in 1892,
architect Irving John Gill, who had worked with
Adler and Sullivan in Chicago, moved away from the
Eclectic style to pioneer new forms and materials.
The serene Women's Club building in La Jolla,
Calif., was a successful example of his experiments
with concrete tilt-slab construction.

Charles Ennis House, 1923 *Above*
This monumental textile-block house by Frank
Lloyd Wright was built on a ridge in Los Angeles six
years after Wright opened an office there. It has a for-
bidding look atypical of Wright's residential
designs—a function of the sheer mass of the walls,
which overpowers both site and viewer in the manner of a Mayan temple.

John Storer House, 1924 *Opposite*
This restored textile-block house is a more successful
example of Wright's work in this mode. Also built in
Los Angeles, it has a sense of grandeur that does not
diminish the occupants. This is the two-story living
room, which extends to a terrace at either end.

Chrysler Building, New York City *Left*

This famous Art Deco skyscraper designed by William Van Alen (1930) is a handsome example of the style, which was popular primarily for public buildings from the mid-1920s through the 1940s. Art Deco commercial buildings are distinguished by stepped-back upper stories; zigzags, chevrons, and other stylized elements as decorative motifs; and spires that accent the vertical thrust. Many attractive examples of Art Deco have been preserved at Florida's Miami Beach, where multicolored, highly decorated hotels rose almost overnight during the heyday of the resort's development.

Cathedral Of Learning, Pittsburgh, Pa. *Opposite*

University architecture responded to contemporary needs in a variety of ways, including the modification of Gothic prototypes, as seen in Charles Klauder's design for the Cathedral of Learning at the University of Pittsburgh (1937).

Cranbrook Academy Of Art, 1941 *Opposite*
Finnish-American architect and planner Eliel
Saarinen was named director of the Cranbrook
Academy of Art in 1925. For twenty-five years, he
developed the complex into one of the nation's premier schools of design. The Academy's reflecting
pool, with sculptures by Carl Miller, is one of the
most attractive features of the Bloomfield Hills,
Mich., campus.

John Deere & Co. Headquarters, 1957 *Above*
Eero Saarinen designed this handsome administration building in Moline, Ill., using Cor-Ten
corrosion-resistant steel. An addition was made in
1963 by architects Kevin Roche John Dinkeloo &
Associates. From 1950, after the death of his father,
Eliel Saarinen, Eero Saarinen worked independently,
designing inventive buildings that reflect his training as a sculptor.

CONTEMPORARY ARCHITECTURE

Frank Lloyd Wright's work was first published abroad, in German, by Ernst Wasmuth in 1910. It was compared to the much-admired work of Josef Maria Olbrich of the Secessionist movement, who was exactly Wright's age, having been born in 1867. European designers were particularly impressed with the rectilinear, hard-edged elements and the functionalism of Wright's style. The look of his buildings coincided with that of Piet Mondrian's post-cubist paintings, in which the Dutch artist sought pure form through a simple geometry that achieved complete abstraction.

German architects Walter Gropius and Ludwig Mies van der Rohe, both born in the 1880s, were motivated by the desire for pure forms that resulted in the Bauhaus—the school of design Gropius founded in Dessau in 1919. Its full name was the Staatliches Bauhaus (State Building School), and the building

Gropius designed for it was the most advanced of its time. It was a new way of stating the principles of Sullivan and Wright—that a building's form should follow its function and that the structure itself should show through. The materials used were glass, steel, and concrete. The major façade formed a kind of cage of glass that extended out from the steel supports and allowed maximum interior light. The clarity, precision, and symmetry of the Bauhaus, with its regular volumes, made it an affirmation of classical principles in the Modern idiom.

When the Nazi Party came to power in Germany, Gropius emigrated to the United States as head of Harvard University's Graduate School of Design. Mies van der Rohe established an American architectural practice with his commission to design a campus and buildings for Chicago's Armour Institute (later the Illinois Institute of Technology). This project occupied him from 1939 until

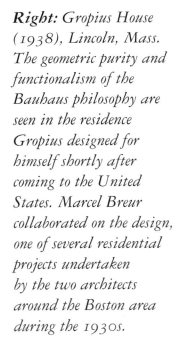

Right: Gropius House (1938), Lincoln, Mass. The geometric purity and functionalism of the Bauhaus philosophy are seen in the residence Gropius designed for himself shortly after coming to the United States. Marcel Breur collaborated on the design, one of several residential projects undertaken by the two architects around the Boston area during the 1930s.

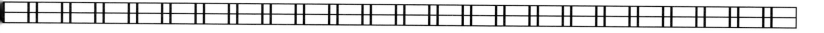

1958, during which time he designed several other notable buildings, including the Lake Shore Apartments in Chicago (1951) and New York City's imposing rectangular Seagram Building (1957), built of bronze and glass and raised on piers in an open space. It has had countless imitators across the country.

Both Gropius and Mies had worked in Europe during the 1910s with the young Swiss architect Charles-Edouard Jenneret, who later practiced in France and became universally known as Le Corbusier. Together with Wright, these four men were widely recognized as the masters of the Modern movement until 1969, when the last of them, Mies and Gropius, died. Gropius had a revolutionizing influence on architectural education in the United States. The philosophy he shared with Mies, Neutra, Schindler, and others was first called the International Style in 1932. In that year, historian and critic Henry-Russell Hitchcock and future architect Philip Cortelyou Johnson published their landmark book of the same title, which predicted that the new style would establish itself around the world.

In 1936 the sixty-nine-year-old Frank Lloyd Wright built his residential masterpiece, Fallingwater, on a wooded site over Bear Run, in western Pennsylvania. Designed for Pittsburgh executive Edgar J. Kaufmann, Sr., it has soaring cantilevered balconies anchored in solid rock and walls of native stone, steel, and glass. Other landmark buildings of Wright's mature period include the Imperial Hotel in Tokyo (1916–22); the Johnson Wax Company Administration Building (1939), in Racine, Wisconsin; the home/studio Taliesin West in Scottsdale, Arizona (1938–1959); the Beth Sholom Synagogue in Elkins Park, Pennsylvania (1954); and the revolutionary Guggenheim Museum in New York City, which has a continuous spiral ramp from which

Left: The influence of the International Style is apparent in this contemporary housing complex, the Esplanade, in Cambridge, Mass. Gropius was the chairman of Harvard University's department of architecture here for fourteen years, during which time he revolutionized architectural education in the United States.

to view the museum's artwork. It rises from an interior court illuminated by a skylight in the domed roof. The building was years in the planning and was completed in 1959, the year of Wright's death. It has since been restored and added to by architects Gwathney Siegel.

Wright's insistence on control over the interior furnishing and design of his buildings sometimes maddened his clients—he was both difficult and demanding—but the results were incomparable, as seen from the Meyer May House of 1908 in Grand Rapids, Michigan, to the Unitarian Church at Shorewood Hills, Wisconsin (1947). The many architects who worked and studied with him throughout his career have made an indelible mark on contemporary architecture, and interest in his design principles has never been more widespread than it is today.

Major American architects who were more deeply influenced by the International Style than by the Wrightian philosophy of organic architecture included several who became prominent in the 1940s and '50s: Philip C. Johnson, Marcel Breuer, Louis Skidmore, Nathaniel Alexander Owings, and John Ogden

year. Other notable commissions included New York City's Lever House (1952), San Francisco's Crown-Zellerbach Building (1958), Chicago's John Hancock Center (1970), and the world's tallest building, the Sears Roebuck Tower, built in Chicago in 1974.

Bauhaus faculty member Marcel Lajos Breuer, a native of Hungary, came to the United States in 1937 to work with Gropius at Harvard and as a partner in his new practice, The Architects' Collaborative. Breuer was primarily a residential architect until the age of fifty. After he set up his own firm, he branched out into other types of buildings, including ecclesiastical and university architecture. In 1958 he designed St. John's Abbey church and college buildings in Collegeville, Minnesota, combining traditional and contemporary materials in a fresh and exciting way. He was associated in this project with Hamilton P. Smith, who also collaborated on the design for New York City's Whitney Museum of American Art (1966). Breuer also practiced abroad, producing an exemplary building for UNESCO in Paris with Bernard H. Zehrfuss and Pier Liugi Nervi (1953–7)

Philip C. Johnson became a force in American architecture even before he took his degree in architecture at Harvard University in 1943, at the age of thirty-seven. As a writer, critic, and lecturer, he had raised public awareness of the International Style. In 1932 he organized the First International Exhibition of Modern Architecture at the influential Museum of Modern Art in New York City, where he was director of the department of architecture. The glass house he designed for himself in New Canaan, Connecticut, in 1949 was instrumental in furthering his reputation after he became a practicing architect. He designed several other houses in New

Above: Beth Shalom Synagogue (1954), in Elkins Park, Pa., was a major work of Frank Lloyd Wright's mature period. He worked closely with the congregation and its rabbi to develop this temple whose form evokes Mount Sinai.

Merrill. The latter three formed a partnership (1939) that became one of the world's largest and most influential architectural firms, with offices in five major cities. Skidmore, Owings and Merrill (SOM) became well known for high-rise office and other public buildings with prefabricated glass- and metal-curtain walls. The firm was chosen to design the U.S. Air Force Academy campus and buildings in Colorado Springs, Colorado, in the early 1960s. Architect Walter Netsch designed the soaring, widely admired Academy Chapel (1963), and SOM's Gordon Bunshaft designed the Beinecke Rare Book and Manuscript Library at Yale University in the same

younger architects, including Michael Graves, Robert A. M. Stern, and Peter Eisenman, all born in the 1930s.

Johnson's distinguished contemporaries included Wallace Kirkman Harrison, Louis Isadore Kahn, and Minoru Yamasaki, each of whom evolved his own distinctive style. Harrison was involved in the design of New York City's Rockefeller Center, the nation's first major architectural complex, which was under construction from 1931 until 1940. Three architectural firms performed the work: Reinhard and Hofmeister; Corbett, Harrison and MacMurray; and Hood and Fouilhoux. Harrison also directed the international team of fifteen architects, including Le Corbusier and Sweden's Sven Markelius, who designed the United Nations Complex along Manhattan's East River (1947–50). During the 1960s, Harrison directed the design and construction of New York's Lincoln Center for the Performing Arts (1962–8). Five other architects contributed to the six-building project, for which Harrison

Top left: The Sears Roebuck Tower (1974), in Chicago, Ill., was designed by Bruce J. Graham of Skidmore, Owings and Merrill. It is the world's tallest building, followed by Minoru Yamasaki's World Trade Center (1973) in New York City.

Canaan during the 1950s, and added two wings to the Museum of Modern Art (1950 and 1964), for which he also designed the sculpture garden (1953).

In 1958 Johnson helped Mies obtain the commission for the Seagram Building, on which he collaborated, and the following decade saw many nonresidential projects. His buildings are sophisticated and boldly conceived, as seen in the Crystal Cathedral (1980) in Anaheim, California, and the Pittsburgh Plate Glass Building of 1984, both the work of Johnson and John Henry Burgee, his partner for twenty years. They also designed the twin towers of Pennzoil Place in Houston, Texas (1976).

Johnson's energy and imagination did not flag even as he entered his eighties. On the contrary, he formed a new architectural firm in 1992, at the age of eighty-six. Only five years before, he had served as the curator of the Museum of Modern Art's exhibition "Deconstructivism in Architecture." Through such exhibitions, and a steady flow of lectures and articles, he advanced the careers of

Left: Marina City, on the Chicago River, was designed by Bertrand Goldberg. Completed in 1961, it is a distinctive multiuse facility including apartments, offices, and shops in two circular towers of concrete construction.

Right: The National Air and Space Museum (1975), in Washington, D.C., was designed by Hellmuth, Obata, and Kassabaum. One of the nation's most popular museums, it shows the influence of Gyo Obata's work with Eliel Saarinen at the Cranbrook Academy of Art and the quality of his design leadership.

designed the Metropolitan Opera House. The others were Philip C. Johnson; Eero Saarinen; Edward Durell Stone; Pietro Belluschi; Skidmore, Owings and Merrill; and Max Abramovitz. Harrison also served as consulting architect on Idlewild (now John F. Kennedy) Airport in Jamaica, New York, a twenty-year project that was completed in 1962.

Louis Isadore Kahn, born in Estonia in 1901, was brought to the United States by his family in 1905 and studied at the Industrial Art School of Philadelphia and the Pennsylvania Academy of Fine Arts. At the University of Pennsylvania's architectural school, during the 1920s, he studied under Paul Philippe Cret. He started his own practice in 1935 and became as well known for his philosophy of architecture as for his buildings, which expressed his convictions about the inherent order in all things and the visible and unseen bonds between them. Much of his time was spent in teaching, study, and contemplation, and he imparted to his students the ideal of an architecture that would serve human needs while achieving a high form of art.

Many of the buildings he designed were never constructed, but their influence was felt by other architects and his students. His best-known works include the Salk Institute for Biological Studies in La Jolla, California (1965), The Kimbell Art Museum in Fort Worth, Texas (1972), and the British Art Center at Yale University, completed in 1976, two years after his death.

Minoru Yamasaki was born in Seattle, Washington, in 1912, the son of Japanese immigrants to the Northwest. As an adolescent, and an honors student, he became fascinated with architecture through the work of his uncle, who was an architect. He studied at the University of Washington and spent eight years in New York City, where the architects he worked with prevented his internment as a Japanese-American during World War II.

After spending three years with the successful Detroit firm of Smith, Hinchman and Grylls, Yamasaki went into practice with Joseph William Leinweber and George F. Hellmuth. They worked together in Detroit from 1949 until 1955, when Hellmuth withdrew to form a new firm in St. Louis. From 1959, Yamasaki headed the firm Minoru Yamasaki and Associates, in Rochester Hills, Michigan.

Yamasaki's style was controversial. Some observers supported his thesis that the social function of an architect is to create a work of art. Others criticized his ornamental forms as capricious, claiming that his buildings were merely decorative. The debate continues at this writing, ten years after his death in 1986.

During his long career, Yamasaki designed more than eighty-five important buildings. Some of the best known are the Reynolds Metal Company Building in Detroit (1960); the Federal Science Pavilion for the World's Fair,

Century 21 in Seattle (1962); the Woodrow Wilson School of Public and International Affairs (1965) at New Jersey's Princeton University; and the twin towers of New York City's World Trade Center (1973), which he designed in association with Emery Roth and Sons.

Architect-émigrés continue to exert an important influence on contemporary American architecture. They include Ulrich Franzen, from Germany; Kevin Roche, from Ireland; Gunnar Birkerts, from Latvia; Cesar Pelli, from Argentina; and Ieoh Ming Pei, who grew up in Shanghai during the 1920s and studied at Harvard University. Exiled from China by the Communist revolution, Pei settled in the United States to become a late Modernist architect of international renown.

Pei worked with Webb and Knapp, directed by developer William Zeckendorf, beginning in 1948. By 1955 his firm—known as I. M. Pei & Associates—was involved in large-scale urban projects. Pei was widely recognized for such designs as the residential complex Society Hill in Philadelphia and the Earth Sciences Building at MIT (both 1964). His commission to design the John F. Kennedy Library, Boston, in 1979, led to other important projects, including the Morton H. Meyerson Symphony Center (1989) in Dallas, Texas, and the Allied Bank Tower, also in Dallas, designed by Pei's partner Henry Cobb.

Pei's recent work continues to reflect his belief that architecture can be monumental without being impersonal. It ranges from the East Wing of the National Gallery (1978) and the Holocaust Museum (1993), both in Washington, D. C., to the glass pyramid added to the venerable Louvre in Paris (1984). The idea provoked outrage at the time, but like many of Pei's buildings, it has become a modern landmark.

The versatile Cesar Pelli, who worked for ten years with Eero Saarinen's firm in Bloomfield Hills, Michigan (1954–63), has moved away from late Modernism since the 1980s to design buildings in new materials and forms more responsive to the past. He has produced important urban and institutional designs including California's San Bernardino City Hall (1972); the Museum of Modern Art Gallery Expansion and Residential Tower (1984), in New York City; the Pacific Design Center, a three-phase project still ongoing in Los Angeles (since 1975); and the Norwest Center in Minneapolis (1989). Since 1977, when he was named dean of Yale University's School of Architecture, Pelli has maintained a New Haven, Connecticut, office with partners Diana Balmori and F. W. Clarke III. Pelli resigned his position at Yale in 1984 to devote more time to his practice.

New directions have been pursued by many other contemporary architects and firms too numerous to list here, despite their important contributions. The following plates include some of their most representative work.

Below: I.M. Pei's Dallas Municipal Administration Center (1977) is one of several impressive projects completed in Texas during the 1970s and '80s. Pei's Morton H. Meyerson Symphony Center (1989) is another Dallas landmark.

Taliesin West, Scottsdale, Ariz. *Above*

Frank Lloyd Wright's mature period saw the inception and development of this home/studio complex in the Southwestern desert, which used native materials including rubblestone and redwood. Massive base walls of desert masonry were surmounted by redwood frames and tentlike canvas coverings. It was built entirely by Wright and his apprentices (1937–59).

S. C. Johnson & Son Research Tower *Right*

Wright made this addition to his milestone commercial complex for the Johnson Wax Company (1936) in Racine, Wisc., in 1949. The streamlined Research Tower is suspended from a treelike metal core that is visible through the translucent walls at night.

Fallingwater, Bear Run, Pa., 1936 *Opposite*

Many consider this beautiful multilevel house cantilevered over a waterfall in western Pennsylvania Wright's masterpiece. It was designed for Pittsburgh department store executive Edgar J. Kaufmann and his family. Edgar J. Kaufmann, Jr., was an apprentice at Taliesin for some time before this commission.

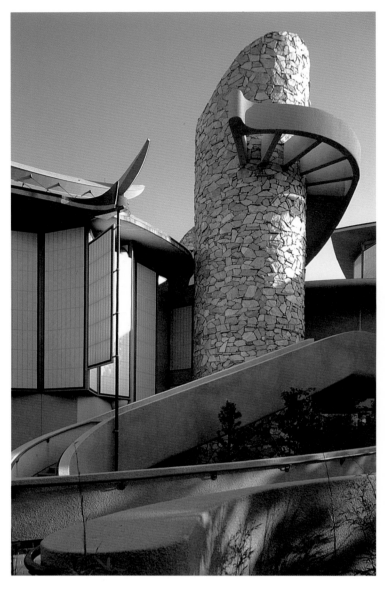

Los Angeles County Museum Of Art *Above*
This contemporary museum was designed by Bruce Goff, a friend and associate of Wright's who shared his passion for organic architecture.

Contemporary Residence, Paul Soldner
Above right (interior) and right (exterior)
The principles of organic architecture are restated in this contemporary house with its sensitive use of native materials, rounded forms, and natural lighting from above.

Watts Towers, Los Angeles, 1921–54 *Opposite*
Artist Simon Rodia produced these soaring pinnacles of welded metal encrusted with shells, tile fragments, and other found objects in what is perhaps the most famous example of American folk art in vernacular building.

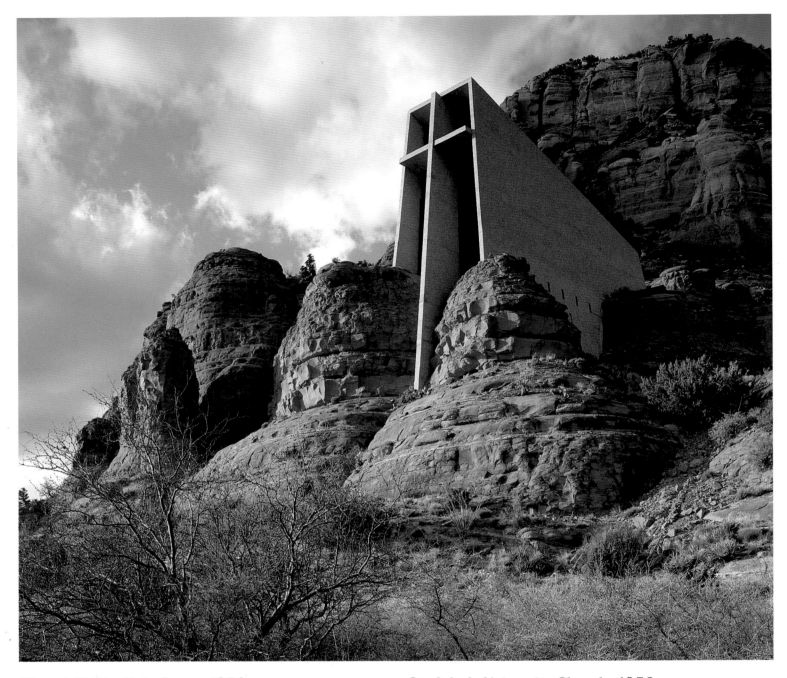

Chapel Of The Holy Cross, 1956 *Above*
Anshen and Allen made a dramatic contemporary
statement in ecclesiastical architecture with this
bold structure that dominates its rugged desert site
in Sedona, Ariz. The verticality of the cross, with
its horizontal beam, unifies the rounded masses
of the ambient landscape into a single striking
composition.

St. John's University Church, 1958 *Opposite*
Hungarian-American architect Marcel Lajos Breuer
designed this impressive concrete structure and other
campus buildings in Collegeville, Minn. Its clean
contemporary lines are strictly of their own time and
reflect the Bauhaus principles shared by Breuer and
Walter Gropius during their long association, first in
Germany and later in the United States.

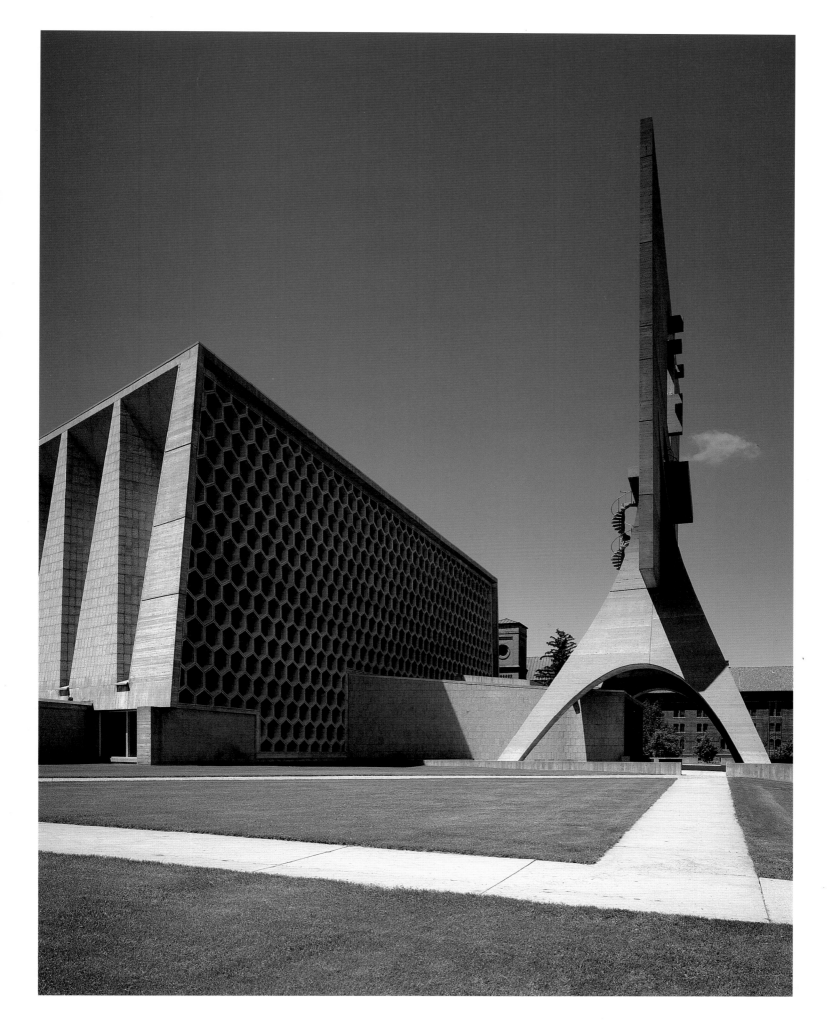

Air Force Academy Chapel, 1963 *Left*

German-born Walter Netsch, of Skidmore, Owings and Merrill, designed the soaring Air Force Academy Chapel after his firm won the coveted commission for the new campus and buildings at Colorado Springs, Colo., in 1962. Netsch was also closely involved with the controversial Chicago Campus of the University of Illinois during the 1960s. Of the Air Force Academy project, he has said: "a ceremonial parade through an open, geometric volume with light streaming through."

Beinecke Rare Book And Manuscript Library *Below*

Gordon Bunshaft of Skidmore, Owings and Merrill used steel, granite aggregate, and white marble for the shell of this impressive library on the Yale University campus in New Haven, Connecticut. Four concrete corner columns give the building the sense of being poised above the plaza.

Priory Chapel, St. Louis, Mo. *Opposite*

Gyo Obata of Hellmuth, Obata and Kassabaum designed the graceful Priory Chapel of St. Mary and St. Louis in 1962. He studied at the Cranbrook Academy of Art with Eliel Saarinen during the 1940s.

Late Modernist I. M. Pei *Below*

The multitiered Rock and Roll Hall of Fame and Museum in Clevelad, Ohio, is one of the most recent additions to Pei's impressive roster of buildings at home and abroad. His skills as an artist and a businessman have placed his firm, Pei, Cobb, Freed and Partners, in the front rank of international architects. His other major works include the East Wing of the National Gallery (1978) in Washington, D.C., and the Dallas Municipal Administration Center (1977) in Dallas, Texas.

Country House, Long Island, N.Y *Opposite*

German-American architect Ulrich Franzen designed this elegant house in East Hampton, a well-known resort for affluent fugitives from Manhattan. Franzen has said that "the most important influence in my life was Mies." His own weekend cottage is in nearby Bridgehampton, Long Island—a streamlined pavilion that floats above the ground on a platform of girders. At this writing, he plans to build another house for himself on a mesa in New Mexico. Franzen has had more than sixty residential commissions.

Philip Johnson "Glass House" *Above*
This Modern milestone was designed and built between 1946 and 1949 in New Canaan, Connecticut, as Johnson's residence. It is entirely transparent except for a cluster of movable shades and built on a brick podium around a brick chimney that penetrates the flat roof plane. The living space is 32 x 56 feet, comprising dining, sitting, and sleeping areas, plus a kitchen counter and the bathroom, within the brick core.

Johnson's Crystal Cathedral, 1980 *Opposite*
Johnson's classic Crystal Cathedral in Anaheim, California, shows his abiding concern with beautiful materials used in imaginative and daring ways. His eminence as an architectural historian is reflected in his designs, which have been called neoclassical. Johnson has said of contemporary architecture, "I do not think we are in a great age of form innovation. The good architecture of this period no doubt has many features of Le Corbusier, Mies, and of other periods, because we are in a consolidating as well as a centrifugal period.... The search is for expression now, rather than for function."

Pittsburgh Plate Glass, Johnson And Burgee *Left*
This towering edifice of glass was completed in 1984 in Pittsburgh, Pa., by Philip Johnson and John Burgee, who worked together for twenty years (1972–92).

Interior, Crystal Cathedral *Below*
A study in light, the Crystal Cathedral brings historic prototypes into contemporary ecclesiastical architecture in a way that has been both praised and criticized by other architects. Johnson has said in another context, "Our culture has not yet created a building comparable to the great public spaces of history. Consider the churches of the Middle Ages— is it religion, or the emotional impact of the great space that moves us?"

Ford Foundation, N.Y.C., Kevin Roche *Right*

Irish-born Kevin Roche, a late Modernist, was influenced by both Mies van der Rohe and Eero Saarinen, whose practice he inherited, with John Dinkeloo, after Saarinen's untimely death in 1961. Perhaps the best-known project of Kevin Roche John Dinkeloo and Associates, the Ford Foundation Headquarters (1968) is an impressive concrete, steel, and glass structure containing an 8,500-foot interior garden.

Salk Institute, Louis Kahn, 1965 *Below*

This austere complex for the Salk Institute for Biological Studies, in La Jolla, Calif., has been called Kahn's masterpiece. Since his death in 1974, his work has been evaluated by critical scholarship as of primary importance to twentieth-century architecture.

Beverly Hills Civic Center, Charles Moore *Above and left*
Architect and educator Charles Moore showed his
appreciation for the Spanish Colonial architecture of
southern California in this attractive complex—a
striking contemporary rendition of regional architec-
ture. Moore taught at both the University of
California at Berkeley and the University of
California at Los Angeles during the 1960s and '70s.
He was also chairman of Yale University's
Department of Architecture from 1965 until 1969.

Pacific Design Center, Cesar Pelli *Above*

This landmark complex was constructed in Los Angeles, Calif., in two phases, 1975 and 1988 (Phase III has been proposed at this writing). The first building houses offices and showrooms in a blue-glazed curtain wall structure; the second is a square green building with truncated corners on a blue base. Both overlook an elegant landscaped courtyard. The proposed Phase III building will be red.

Norwest Center, 1989, Cesar Pelli *Right*

This impressive commercial center in Minneapolis, Minn., designed by Cesar Pelli and Associates, shows how the firm has moved from late Modernism into materials and forms that are more responsive to historic buildings of the early twentieth century. The interior of the Norwest Bank has a great paneled vault with clerestory windows, a painted dome, and leaded-glass chandeliers.

San Juan Capistrano Library, Michael Graves *Left*

Post-Modern architect Michael Graves designed this widely admired public building in 1982 in San Juan Capistrano, Calif. His study of the Spanish Mission style resulted in organization around an internal court, with roofed outdoor reading areas and covered walkways. The exterior is in keeping with local architecture, utilizing cream-colored stucco and red tile roofs.

The Humana Building, 1985, Louisville, Ky *Bottom left*

Michael Graves designed this dramatic building with projected terrace and conference room at the 26th-floor level for a site near the Ohio River. It is transitional between neighboring structures—low older buildings nearby and the high-rise towers of downtown Louisville.

High Museum Of Art, Richard Meier *Opposite top*

Atlanta, Ga., is the site of this 1983 museum of art, which has a central sky-lit atrium and curving ramps that provide access to the upper floors. Exhibition spaces are on adjoining galleries. Meier acknowledges Le Corbusier and Frank Lloyd Wright as his major inflences.

California Aerospace Museum, Los Angeles

Opposite bottom

Deconstructivist Frank O. Gehry turned to art-centered design early in his career, as seen in this striking museum for Los Angeles, Calif. (1984). Several of his other museums have been highly commended, including the Frederick R. Weisman Museum of Art (1993) at Minnesota's University of Minneapolis.

Timeless Twentieth-Century Designs *Left and right*
Current trends in architecture favor retaining the best of historic forms and enhancing them through fresh interpretations and improved technology. The early modern Chicago town house opposite, designed by Dirk Dennison, is an excellent example of this melding of historic influences and modern technology. Open space, ample light, and economy of line make it a contemporary urban home in keeping with Chicago's impressive history in American and world architecture.

The Southwestern vernacular is expressed in the contemporary-feeling residence at right (above), with its traditional corner fireplace of adobe painted with Native American symbols. Note the tile ornamentation at the base of the fireplace and above the deeply recessed window. The bold organic forms of the concrete façade at Pedregal Plaza (right, below), in Scottsdale, Arizona, with its brightly painted openings and pierced wall, recall pre-Columbian architecture. This complex rises powerfully from the desert lanscape in a series of smooth-surfaced buildings overlooking an architectural landscape of native plants.

GLOSSARY OF ARCHITECTURAL TERMS

The following brief definitions cover architectural terms used in this book:

architrave: the lowermost part of an entablature, resting directly on top of a column in classical architecture

balustrade: row of miniature columns (balusters) supporting a handrail, often used decoratively to frame or crown porches

batten: a narrow strip of wood used especially for flooring and siding

belt course: a change of exterior material of pattern marking the stories of a building

buttress: masonry pier used for reinforcement of walls

capital: the top part or head of a pillar or column

cantilever: a projecting beam or other structure supported at only one end

casement window: a narrow window with sashes that open outward on hinges

cladding: material used to cover the structural elements of a building exterior

colonnade: row of columns with horizontal entablature

corbel: masonry block projecting from wall to support a horizontal feature

cornice: projecting feature at top of walls, arches, and other structural elements

dentil: one of a series of small rectangular blocks forming a molding or projecting beneath a cornice

dogtrot: a roofed passage between two parts of a building

dormer window: vertically positioned window set in a sloping roof

eave: see gable

entablature: the upper section of a classical order, resting on the capital and including the architrave, frieze, and cornice

fanlight: a half-circle window, often with sash bars arranged like the ribs of a fan

finial: vertical ornament fixed to the peak of an arch or arched structure

fretwork: ornamental feature consisting of thru-dimensional geometric designs or other symmetrical figures (frets) enclosed in a band or border

friezeboard: decorative band around a wall

gable: triangular area enclosed by the edges of a sloping roof. The gable ends of a building are the walls under the gables (usually at the sides); the eave ends are the walls underneath the faces of a sloping roof

gambrel roof: ridged roof with two slopes on each side, the lower slope having the steeper pitch

half-timbering: type of timber frame construction in which the surfaces between posts and beams are filled in with another material while the timber remains visible

hip: the external angle formed by the meeting of two adjacent sloping sides of a roof

jetty: a second story projecting over the first-story façade

lintel: horizontal beam or stone placed over door or window openings

mansard: a roof with a double slope on all four sides, the lower slope being steeper than the upper (for the 17th-century French architect François Mansard)

modillion: small bracket supporting a cornice

mullion: vertical window division (*see* transom)

ogee arch: an arch of two curves melting at a point, as in Oriental architecture; also, a double curve with the shape of an elongated S

oriel window: upper-story bay window supported by a corbel or bracket

parapet: a low wall or railing along the edge of a roof or balcony

pediment: triangular feature over a portico, consisting of horizontal entablature with sloping cornice edges

pier: supporting post or stone, often square, thicker than a column

pilaster: shallow pier attached to a wall, usually rectangular, for decoration and/or reinforcement

portico: colonnaded entry porch

post-and-girt construction: timber framing joined by hand-hewn notches

quoins: patterned stonework at the corners of a building and/or façade opening like windows and doors

sidelight: narrow windows flanking a doorway

siding: boards, shingles, or other material used to surface a frame building

stickwork: exterior patterned woodwork that serves an ornamental rather than a structural purpose

stucco: a durable finish for exterior walls, applied wet and usually composed of cement, sand, and lime

tab: stone used to form ornamental patterns in masonry façades

transom: horizontal window division (*see* mullion) or opening above a window or door

vault: arched roof or ceiling

INDEX

ACKNOWLEDGEMENTS

The publisher would like to thank the following for their contributions to this book: Emily Elizabeth Head for preparing the index; Jim Kahnweiler for assistance with graphic design; Annie Lise Roberts for her advice; the individuals and institutions who gave permission for the reproduction of their photographs. All photographs are copyright © by Balthazar Korab except as listed below:

© Carla Breeze (pages 94, 141 top); Corel (pages 8 bottom, 41 bottom, 49, 50, 55 bottom, 57 bottom right, 60, 62, 64, 65 bottom, 66 top); © Jim Kahnweiler (pages 17, 33 top, 35 top, 71, 117, 124 top right and bottom); Museum of New Mexico (page 29, photo by T. Harmon Parkhurst, # 12505); Nebraska State Historical Society, Solomon Butcher Collection (page 28); Prints and Photographs Division, Library of Congress (pages 7 top, 12, 27); The Southwest Museum, Los Angeles (page 6 top, # CT 518 MCC.288); © Charles Ziga (endpapers).